Small Beginnings,
BIG Future

Unlikely

Candidate

MY IMPROBABLE ADVENTURE
THROUGH DELINQUENCY AND
LIFE-DEFINING TWISTS TO
BECOMING A CHICK-FIL-A OWNER

David Grimm

Prepared for publication by www.40DayPublishing.com

Cover design by www.40DayGraphics.com

Printed in the United States of America

Table of Contents

Dedication

This book is dedicated to my Lord and Savior, Jesus Christ, who makes everything possible. Without His divine intervention, this story—and perhaps my ability to tell any story—would not exist. Though the lessons were hard and the journey often painful, I am forever grateful for His interruptions in my life. The suffering was a part of the process, and I've learned that enduring the pain is always worth the outcome if you don't give up. *Galatians 6:9.*

Introduction: Discovering More

If you've ever felt like an outcast or like you're just another face in the crowd, I wrote this book for you. I've been there too, and I understand the pain and isolation that comes with it.

I remember Day One of first grade as if it were yesterday. The school was crowded, full of kids running and laughing in the main waiting area as the buses began to arrive.

Even though it was the end of summer, the room felt cold – at least it did to me. Everything was unfamiliar. I had no idea what to expect and didn't know any of my fellow classmates. I sat among a large group of students but still felt alone. I can't understate the relief I felt when a lone third grader walked over to me to say hi. It only took one interaction to feel like I was no longer isolated. Perhaps this would be the start of an excellent elementary school experience.

We were dismissed to class. After the daily pledge of allegiance and prayer, we opened the books to our first subject: math. Although I had attended a self-paced school the year before as a kindergarten student, I had no memory of learning anything about math. Eventually, that school would shut down due to various factors, one of which was insufficient educational guidance that resulted in a failure to equip students with the essential knowledge needed for future academic success.

I was completely lost once the teacher began explaining basic math principles. I had never seen problems like this before, so you can imagine my apprehension when the teacher called me to the front of the class to solve an equation on the chalkboard. Although I had no idea what I was doing, I attempted to solve the problem anyway.

My answer must have been incorrect because my teacher initially responded, "Are you stupid?" Immediately, any sense of trust I had in this teacher evaporated, and the class began roaring with laughter. In case it's not clear, they were laughing *at* me, not *with* me. Decades later, I still can't comprehend what would lead an adult to say that to a child.

I carried that shame with me for the rest of the year. I was never able to trust that teacher again. So much for the superior start I was hoping for in school. That encounter left an indelible mark on my self-esteem, and the experience impacted me for years to come.

However, it's not the identity I carry today. Praise God for His ability to repurpose broken pieces into a beautiful mosaic. As God tells Jeremiah (even after foreshadowing the exile of the Israelites to Babylon), "'For I know the plans I have for you,' says the Lord. 'They are plans for good and not for disaster, to give you a future and a hope.'" (Jeremiah 29:11, NLT)

Have you ever felt weak or insignificant? Do you carry a sense of insecurity or inadequacy because you aren't the best-looking, the most intelligent, or the most talented? If you can relate to any of these descriptions, you're in good company. I've been there too. For years, this was my life.

What was most difficult was that I didn't know I was living this way at first. I know it's hard to understand, but hindsight is 20/20. Looking back on my earlier years, I realize that I was living with an unconscious sense of my lack of self-worth. It was impacting my life in a significant way. Although I could identify the symptoms, I was unaware of the root cause. As I've grown older and faced different circumstances and experiences, I've developed a lens to view my childhood that allows me to look back and understand what I was going through. Even though I've always heard that comparison is a trap, this comparison was beneficial for me because it helped me make sense of how things really were at a time when I was struggling.

Ultimately, you can't control where - or if - you're born, and some of us are certainly dealt a more brutal hand from the beginning. However, God has a unique way of taking obstacles and turning them into opportunities. God often reveals His power most prominently through our deepest pain points. As Paul writes in 1 Corinthians 1:26-27 (NLT), "Remember, dear brothers and sisters, that few of you were wise in the world's eyes or powerful or wealthy when God called you. Instead, God chose things the world considers foolish in order to shame those who think they are wise. And he chose things that are powerless to shame those who are powerful."

I'm so grateful that I serve a God who can do extraordinary things with what the world says is weak and foolish. By all metrics, I am an unlikely candidate for the tremendous success I've been blessed to experience. My interviewers always said, "David, you look horrible on paper." My prospects have never been all that bright. Still, somehow, God has led me down an incredible path that He charted out before I was even born. He crafted a plan that enabled me to stand out against thousands of candidates who were more qualified than me. Despite all the evidence I had that said I was insufficient and that I didn't stack up, the only standard of true significance was how God saw me. In other words, all that mattered was that God said I mattered.

I believe the same is true for you. God sees tremendous, immeasurable value in you regardless of your background, appearance, perceived intelligence, socioeconomic status, geographical location, physical abilities, family circumstances, or any other factors. You may not believe it yet, but I'm fully convinced that when you wholeheartedly surrender your life to God and invite Him into your everyday existence, you'll quickly find that when God is present, anything is possible. As Jesus said, "'The things which are impossible with men are possible with God.'" (Luke 18:27, NKJV)

If you've ever felt like an unlikely candidate on an improbable journey, there's a good chance that God is laying the groundwork to do something extraordinary in your life. At the same time, discovering your true worth and the value God has bestowed on you is no easy task. We all face obstacles in life, and whether they are

iv

external or internal, the process of overcoming them is arduous and messy. It could take years of persistence, upward motion, and allowing God to cleanse and refine you before you finally reach a significant milestone on your journey.

That said, the challenges may be daunting, but the rewards are exponential and eternal. If your deepest desire is to fulfill God's purpose in your life and experience more of His presence, you've picked up the right book. My story of triumph and transformation could be yours as well if you're willing to say "yes" to God's calling and take steps forward in your faith – especially when that means embracing the uncomfortable and the unknown. The abundant life waiting for you on the other side makes all the sacrifices worth it.

It's time to give the broken pieces of your heart that you've been carrying with you over to God. He just might be getting ready to do something extraordinary with them! Are you prepared to embark on a journey to discover what God's plan for your life could be?

> *"The thief does not come except to steal, and to kill, and to destroy. I have come that they may have life, and that they may have it more abundantly."*
>
> John 10:10 NKJV

Chapter One: Home

My odds of winning an opportunity were only 0.0017%. Statistically speaking, I had a better chance of being struck by lightning or becoming a professional athlete. These were not encouraging odds, but they were the odds I was up against, and if this was what I was meant to pursue, I was determined to beat them.

As I sat in the waiting room, the air was thick with anticipation. The thousands of applicants I was up against seemed to loom over me. My mind wandered back to my first visit to the Chick-fil-A Corporate Headquarters in Atlanta (now called the Support Center). I recalled the franchisee brochure I saw on the table as I waited to be called back to the room for one of my first in-person interviews. I resisted the urge to open it, not wanting to be discouraged by the slim chances it revealed. I held onto the faith and hope that God had put in my heart.

Two and a half years later (and more than 12 rounds of interviews), we made it to the ultimate stage. Our hands tightly clasped together, I sat beside my wife, Kelly, who had walked with me and supported me throughout the journey. At that moment, she was just as nervous as me. As we waited outside the interviewer's office, we heard rumors that cameras and microphones captured every word we uttered and every move we made.

We laughed nervously. We were still in disbelief that we had made it this far. A quick scan of the room showed no evidence of any hidden cameras, and we were able to relax slightly. Perhaps they were just hidden exceptionally well.

After what seemed like hours, the time finally arrived. Our palms sweating, we grabbed each others' hands tighter and prayed before we were called back into the office for the interview. Initially, I felt like I was back in high school and being called into the principal's office for discipline. [1] Deep down, I knew this wasn't a punishment but a chance for our lives to change forever.

Kelly and I sat at a round table across from the interviewer. Briefly, this man explained that his role was to guard the interests of the Cathy family. In case you aren't familiar with Truett Cathy, he founded Chick-fil-A in 1946. He then opened the conversation with a simple prompt: "Tell me about your life."

I was instantly taken aback. Although I was prepared to answer many questions at that moment, this was not one of them. Where should I even begin? My mind raced as I tried to decide which parts of my life were the most important to share, which experiences had shaped me the most, and how to condense it all into a coherent and compelling story.

---

[1] I mean, I assume it would feel like this. I've obviously never been called back to the principal's office myself! (Keep reading and you'll quickly understand that this is sarcasm)

I began to tell a story from when I was 17 years old. I was facing jail time, and my life took a dramatic turn. This was a significant defining moment for me, and I thought this story could lead to a discussion about why I was pursuing this opportunity. It was during this time that I found my faith, a faith that has guided me through the ups and downs of life, and a faith that I believe has brought me to this moment.

"Wait a minute," the interviewer cut me off mid-sentence. "We just skipped a huge section of your life. Let's go back to the beginning."

I was caught off guard again. "The beginning? Like when I was born?" I responded.

"Yeah, that seems like a good place to start," the interviewer commented.

"Okaaaay..." I drew out the word slowly as I contemplated how to summarize the previous 35 years of my life to this man in the allotted one-hour interview. Sixty minutes isn't much time, but the words I shared in these brief moments could make or break my opportunity and change the course of my family history. Throughout my life, I have learned to pray a simple prayer often, especially in critical moments like this.

"God, give me wisdom."

I silently prayed this prayer as I began speaking.

Humble Beginnings

I was born in a Western Pennsylvanian town called Somerset. We then lived in the nearby town of Berlin. This is the same town where they make the delicious "Snyder of Berlin" potato chips. If you've never tried them, I highly recommend you pick up a bag next time you're at the store. They're now more commonly known as "Utz."

My earliest memories were as a two-year-old in the Appalachian Mountains of Somerset County. I remember living in a tiny trailer next to the small church. My dad was a pastor at the rural country church. I can still recall picnics at the pavilion on the property, where I would throw a football back and forth with my friends as my parents visited with other church members.

My dad only spent a few years in full-time ministry, but this short stint still impacted his life. He often told me, "David, don't go into ministry unless you know God is calling you to do it. It won't work if He hasn't." I took these words to heart because I knew if my dad was concerned enough about my future to give me this unsolicited wisdom, the ministry might be a difficult and draining occupation. His advice has guided me through many decisions and challenges, reminding me to always seek God's will and not my own.

Ironically, most people would have never imagined a future in ministry for me based on how my life was going at the time. Perhaps my dad also had an intuition about what might happen to me later in life. Still, this intuition was vastly different from how most people perceived me. My friend's dad told him not to hang out with me anymore. He was sure I'd end up dead or in jail and didn't want his son to end up like me. Thankfully, God had different plans.

Of course, I'm skipping over a vital part of this story (if the interviewer from Chick-fil-A was listening in, he would have already cut me off and redirected me). After my dad's brief pastoral experience, we moved about 40 miles west to my grandparent's house on my mother's side. They lived in a small town called Latrobe, PA, about an hour's drive from where we were living previously. My father was now a Christian retail and bookstore manager, and my parents' desire to save money to buy a home brought us to the area.

Latrobe may be small, but it has character. The first banana split was invented at the local Strickler's Drug Store, and the first professional football game was played in town. Arnold Palmer - both the professional golfer and the popular beverage - can trace their roots back to Latrobe. So can Fred Rogers, the host of the renowned children's television show "Mr. Roger's Neighborhood," which primarily aired in the 1960's. To this day, the NFL's Pittsburgh Steelers hold their annual training camp in Latrobe, and you could even walk to their summer practices on a trail between my childhood house and nearby Saint Vincent College.

For the next 31 years, Latrobe would be my home. As a young child, I had no idea how much time I would spend in this community or what a critical role this town would play in my story.

What Heaven Feels Like

It's hard for me to imagine Heaven without envisioning my grandparents' farm. This special place will always feel like home to me. In my mind, I can still go back to their old, overclad log cabin with cedar paneling anytime I want to tap back into some of my most cherished memories.

Their home was an old Revolutionary War cabin called Lochry's Blockhouse, where my Italian "grandpap," Anthony Todaro, tilled the fields seasonally to plant his corn and other crops. As he moved through the fields, he would collect arrowheads and place them in a shoebox. In the early days, battles between early settlers and Native Americans would often occur on the grounds near what is now the Lincoln Highway. Their homestead oozed history, and I was blessed to call this place "home" from ages two to six.

While my Grandpap worked the fields, I would play in the woods near the cabin on abandoned railroad tracks. I would climb the same apple trees in the orchard where my Grandpap would harvest apples each fall to make cider. Each morning, I would feed the chickens in the coop, pick eggs, and run through the grape arbors, where Grandpap would harvest grapes to make homemade wines and jellies.

Soon after, the smell of Grandma Anna's cooking would draw me back into the house. Most people knew her better by her affectionate nickname, "Bubba." My Slovakian grandma would regularly make fresh eggs and coffee, homemade pasta, donuts, baked goods, haluski, and other ethnic favorites that filled the kitchen and dinner table each day.

Of course, all the delicious food in the world wouldn't mean much if you couldn't share it with friends, family, and loved ones. My grandparents were the most hospitable people I've ever known, and they taught my parents to uphold the same values. Our home was always open to others going through a hard season or unable to support themselves.

My grandmother constantly fed the homeless as they made their way down the old nearby mining railroad. We would often have neighbors stop by for a quick afternoon visit that turned into an invitation to join us for dinner and a bottle of Grandpap's homemade wine. We spent many weeknights hosting relatives for meals, games, and laughter later into the night. I thoroughly enjoyed watching them play and even tried to learn some games myself. I quickly learned how to spot my grandpap cheating. I always loved watching him laugh uncontrollably as my grandma reprimanded him.

I would sit on my grandma's lap every morning to watch cartoons or gameshows. Afterward, we would eat breakfast together, and I would steal sips of her coffee. My addiction began when I was young, and I haven't stopped loving coffee ever since. I often think of my grandma when I enjoy my favorite beverage.

The days would end with prayers and my parents tucking me into bed in my corner room at the top of the wooden staircase. I would stay awake until my parents' bedroom door shut, so I knew it was safe to sneak downstairs to watch Johnny Carson on The Tonight Show with my grandparents. Of course, Mom and Dad would quickly discover that I wasn't in bed, and my escapade would promptly end.

I could tell you so much more about the nostalgic feelings of this place I remember fondly. I could talk all day about watching animals by the freshwater spring, picking fresh berries and vegetables in the garden, or planting flower beds in the greenhouse. I recall spending time shopping at the Jamesway department store (where my grandma would always buy me a treat) or eating lunch at the Jamesway diner with my mom and grandma. I could think back on all the chores I helped Grandpap with on the farm. Although it doesn't sound like fun, there were few (if any) activities I would rather be doing.

Looking back, I'm grateful for this season of my life and the memories that blur together into a tapestry of carefree perfection. At the time, everything felt endless. I rejoice today because even though this particular season of my life is over, the memories give me a picture of the sense of home I hope we all experience together in Heaven one day.

Eternal Longing

These memories remind us of something we all feel deep down: a longing for a place where we truly belong, where life thrives free from fear and limitations. This explains why I still sometimes have dreams of living there. I long to return where everything is full of life and free of restriction.

This profound yearning for a true sense of home and belonging stems from my upbringing. Growing up in the warm embrace of my grandparents' farm – where the bonds of family, community, and love were woven into everyday life – I understood that "home" extends far beyond the physical structure. Home is a state of heart and mind where we can fully embrace our true selves. These early experiences ignited a lifelong journey to recreate that same essence of home in every corner of my life. As the Teacher writes in Ecclesiastes 3:11 (NLT), "He has planted eternity in the human heart..."

The ancient wisdom of Ecclesiastes echoes the profound truth that our hearts carry an eternal seed of longing. Looking back at the laughter-filled days on my grandparent's farm, I can't help but see that those fleeting moments were like glimpses of eternity, where time stood still and joy overflowed. It's as if my soul recognized that this world, with all its transitory beauty, was but a shadow of the true home where we were created to live. The essence of our existence bears witness to a reality that stretches beyond the finite and whispers of something more.

God has built in all of us an eternal capacity and longing. Intrinsically, we know there's something more beyond this present life. Even when we refuse to acknowledge it, we can't shake the deep, internal hope of something more. We all know we were created for something beyond what we are presently experiencing. We all have a God-shaped hole in our hearts that can only be filled by a relationship with Him. The only way to begin that relationship is through His only Son, Jesus Christ. In Jesus, we find this innate longing truly fulfilled. When we put our hope and trust in Jesus, the ache in our hearts is satisfied, and our joy is made whole.

John 3:16 is one of the most famous passages in Scripture, and for good reason. These profound words contain a tremendous promise for each person who puts their trust in Jesus. John 3:16-17 (NKJV) reads, "For God so loved the world that He gave His only begotten Son, that whoever believes in Him should not perish but have everlasting life. For God did not send His Son into the world to condemn the world, but that the world through Him might be saved."

No matter how much we may try to deny it, any choice or pursuit in this life will only leave us longing and hurting for more unless a relationship with Jesus is at its core. Nothing finite can fill the space designed to be occupied by only the infinite. Only God alone can satisfy this void. The sooner we stop fighting this reality and trying to satisfy our longings with everything the world has to offer, the sooner we can begin living the life God intends us to enjoy. You may wonder why I'm so confident in this belief, but you'll quickly learn as we continue our story.

Today, my grandparent's cabin is a preserved relic safeguarded by the historical society. However, the wonderful life I lived there and the joy I experienced have faded from plain sight, leaving only precious memories etched into the passage of time. The plowed fields are gone. The gardens and grape arbors are grown over. The apple trees are still alive, but my grandpap isn't harvesting for cider anymore. The physical location may be the same when I take my wife and kids back to visit, but the experience is vastly different. The past is temporary, but the memories live forever.

Not everyone grew up in the same way that I did. Perhaps thinking about your upbringing brings up painful memories and negative feelings. If that's your experience, I want you to know how sorry I am. I empathize entirely with you, but I know your true "home" still awaits you. In addition, you still have an opportunity to create a beautiful environment for yourself on this side of Heaven. The specific surroundings may differ from what others are experiencing, but you can still cultivate a meaningful sense of "home."

God desires everyone to experience an abundant life and a deep sense of belonging. I know this because of Jesus' words in John 10 when He tells His disciples that the thief comes to steal, kill, and destroy, but He has come "that they may have life and that they may have it more abundantly." (John 10:10, NKJV)

We live in a fallen world with a genuine enemy who would love nothing more than to rob us of these blessings. His ultimate goal is to prevent us from experiencing the highest possible goodness, both in this life and in the next life. This is why many homes are broken and lack a true sense of belonging. The enemy's objective is to destroy what God has created for good, but God ultimately has different aspirations for us. The same promise God makes to Jeremiah in Jeremiah 29:11 is true for us: "For I know the thoughts that I think toward you, says the Lord, thoughts of peace and not of evil, to give you a future and a hope." (Jeremiah 29:11, NKJV)

God's plans for us are good, even if they don't always feel that way in the moment. God promises that if we put our faith in Him and give Him the broken pieces of our lives, He will make something miraculous out of the fragments and loose ends. God has the power to remake us, and He's willing to step in if we allow Him the space to go to work.

As this first chapter ends, I'll leave you with the words of Paul in Romans 8:28 (NIV): "And we know that in all things God works for the good of those who love him, who have been called according to his purpose."

I've had to learn how to trust God's promises as I submit my broken pieces to Him. You may feel completely shattered, but God can put you back together and make you whole. If you submit to His plans, you'll quickly find that the new picture is more beautiful than anything that existed before.

Chapter Two: Authoritarian Abuse

Growing up in my neighborhood was a tremendous experience until the day I faced an undesired and unexpected encounter. Looking back, I should have been more cautious because I wasn't fully prepared for what was about to unfold. If I knew then what I know now, I would have understood how deeply our sense of home impacts our personality and character. I could have seen that my values would erode by spending too much time in a place where they weren't shared, honored, or upheld. However, I was too young and naive to see that not everyone had the same tremendous upbringing as me.

My grandparents, generous as they were, had just allotted an acre of land for my family near their property. My dad was always incredibly industrious and handy, so he constructed our home over time from scratch using materials he bought himself. By my sixth birthday, we lived in the space that would eventually become our home's basement.

It took my dad four years to compile enough cash to build the rest of our home. This didn't bother me because I considered living underground an adventure akin to having my own secret lair. While living in the basement, my sister Charity joined our small family, making us a family of four. We later added to our household again when we welcomed a new Chihuahua-Terrier mix dog named "Friskey." I loved that little dog!

The joy of exploring the farm and the unique experience of living in an underground house filled my childhood with excitement and adventure. As an adventurous young boy, I couldn't have asked for more.

Still, my world changed for the better when refugees from Laos arrived on our property in search of sanctuary from the despotism and atrocities taking place in their home country. Sponsored by family friends, they were granted permission by my grandparents to set up a trailer on our land. Suddenly, I had three new children my age to play with daily.

Despite the language barrier, we formed instant connections and exchanged toys.

Beyond the companionship, I also had the opportunity to experience a new cuisine. The spicy watercress flourished in the nearby cold spring water, and flying cicadas added an exotic touch. I never mustered the courage to try the cicadas, but I loved everything about the experience (hot peppers included).

Unfortunately, the good times wouldn't last. The changes began when my Laotian neighbors and newfound friends decided to relocate. I had grown attached to the three children and was sad to see them go.

As much as they left a void in my life when they moved, this loss paled in comparison to the loss of my grandparents. With their departure, the vibrant life that unfolded next door and the countless adventures it offered became a memory. The undeniable truth is that change is an integral facet of life's journey. We lost my grandpap first. After his death, I began visiting my grandma daily to keep her company, as she now lived alone.

When I walked in one day for our regular visit, she sat at her writing desk, finishing a phone conversation. Tragically, she fell as she stood up to greet me. The fall left her with a broken arm and a deep gash in her head. I immediately ran next door to alert my mother, who called 911. Unfortunately, the damage was done, and my grandma joined my grandpap shortly after her fall.

With their departure, my paradise was gone. My blissful reality on the farm was now only a memory. Knowing that my world would never exist the way it did before left me feeling sad and empty.

My grandparents had left, but my longing for adventure was as intense as ever. As I grew older, I began exploring further out into the neighborhood. We lived at the end of the street, a brisk walk down the long gravel driveway from my grandparents' farm. After you passed my home, you reached the rest of the neighborhood. This space was called St. Vincent Shaft, named after the mineshafts where coal miners worked and lived years before. Traces of the old mining neighborhood were still evident, with pieces of coal littered all over the landscape in the woods below our houses and on the old railroad tracks that were no longer in use. Periodic sinkholes would reveal themselves when a shaft collapsed deep underground. The mining company built the other homes in our "shaft" neighborhood, intended for two families to live in.

These homes were called duplexes, where I discovered more kids my age. The more time I spent in St. Vincent Shaft, the more friends I made. Back in those days, everyone participated in raising each other's children. We were in and out of each other's houses daily – especially in the summer. Sometimes, we got to eat two dinners if someone invited us to stay. We ate with our friends first and then went home to eat a second time with our family. Honestly, I miss those two-dinner nights! More so, I miss being able to eat like this without gaining an ounce.

As time passed and we grew older, our interests evolved. The days of exploring the woods and riding bikes were replaced by new fascinations. We were now into video games with the dawn of the Nintendo and all the other video game consoles soon to follow. Amidst these changes, the allure of cable TV entered our lives, diverting our attention from the adventures we once cherished.

With the families being as caring as they were back then, and because many of our parents also grew up together, everyone was very trusting. The same is probably true for many parents today, but my warning to every parent is to be cautious. You shouldn't trust everyone because they seem "nice" and come from a "good" family. Even if your family is friends with their family, a slight degree of caution is still appropriate. Your kids soak up words and experiences like sponges; their minds and hearts are vulnerable. Not everyone should be trusted with your children; first impressions can sometimes be misleading. This lesson, learned through my own experiences, is a reminder of the importance of vigilance and understanding in parenting.

Unwanted Influences

You don't always choose what happens to you, but you get to decide how you respond to every circumstance. In addition, you can make intelligent choices in advance to limit or avoid some unwanted events for you and the people you love. We must be careful and wise about the influences we allow to infiltrate our hearts and minds. Remember, a tiny seed can grow into a large plant when watered and nurtured, even if it turns out to be a weed. When we allow these weeds to develop, we risk choking out the most good and fruitful plants in the gardens of our hearts and minds. As we read in Proverbs 4:23 (NLT), "Guard your heart above all else, for it determines the course of your life."

I didn't understand the importance of protecting my heart at the time. I didn't know anything besides my innocence, and I wasn't prepared for it to be stripped away from me and replaced with something I never should have witnessed. I thought I could trust a particular friend's family. Still, this trust quickly eroded as I began to see explicit scenes flash across their TV screen. Horrific portrayals of sex and violence were suddenly etched into my young mind, a gallery of unsettling images and fantasies that produced fear and invoked dark thoughts. Before setting foot in this home, I had never listened to explicit music or heard about witchcraft or demonic influences. I hadn't opened an inappropriate magazine until I saw every dirty picture in my friend's father's collection. I even learned how to smoke cigarettes by lighting up my friend's grandma's stash.

Make no mistake - this home was nothing like our home. They didn't share our values. They had few - if any - noticeable boundaries. Because of my time in this space, my mind was forever altered at a young age. My innocence would never return, and my life had drastically changed.

I could have run, but I didn't. I chose not to tell my parents. Instead, I returned for more. I came back repeatedly, and my heart grew colder and darker each time.

War

Every day, we face competing desires. We want to lose weight, but we also want to eat a cheeseburger for lunch. We want to pray and read our Bibles, but instead, we binge-watch our favorite TV shows or scroll endlessly through our social media feeds.

You're not alone if your actions don't always match your ultimate desires. In Romans 7, the apostle Paul famously speaks about his propensity to do the things he would prefer not to do. "I have discovered this principle of life—that when I want to do what is right, I inevitably do what is wrong. But there is another power within me that is at war with my mind. This power makes me a slave to the sin that is still within me. Oh, what a miserable person I am! Who will free me from this life that is dominated by sin and death? Thank God! The answer is in Jesus Christ our Lord. So you see how it is: In my mind I really want to obey God's law, but because of my sinful nature I am a slave to sin." (Romans 7:21, 23-25, NLT)

Paul, an apostle of Jesus Christ, perfectly captures the war waging within each of us. We all are meant to live a life full of purity and goodness, but when sin enters, it begins an internal war for our souls. This will be an ever-present battle until we are no longer here on this earth, and the blood of Jesus Christ is the only thing that can ensure our victory.

Something powerful happens when we accept the grace and salvation that only comes from a relationship with Jesus. Paul expands on the impact of Jesus' crucifixion in Romans 6:

> *"We know that our old sinful selves were crucified with Christ so that sin might lose its power in our lives. We are no longer slaves to sin. For when we died with Christ we were set free from the power of sin. And since we died with Christ, we know we will also live with him. We are sure of this because Christ was raised from the dead, and he will never die again. Death no longer has any power over him. When he died, he died once to break the power of sin. But now that he lives, he lives for the glory of God. So you also should consider yourselves to be dead to the power of sin and alive to God through Christ Jesus. Do not let sin control the way you live; do not give in to sinful desires. Do not let any part of your body become an instrument of evil to serve sin. Instead, give yourselves completely to God, for you were dead, but now you have new life. So*

use your whole body as an instrument to do what is right for the glory of God. Sin is no longer your master, for you no longer live under the requirements of the law. Instead, you live under the freedom of God's grace."

(Romans 6:6-14, NLT)

Since I was introduced to the destruction of sin many years ago, I have learned how to wage this war. As much as we may feel we are victims of our circumstances, we don't have to remain in victimhood. We can choose to forgive those who have wronged us, just as the Father freely forgives us. In the book of Colossians, Paul commands, "Make allowance for each other's faults, and forgive anyone who offends you. Remember, the Lord forgave you, so you must forgive others."(Colossians 3:13, NLT)

This doesn't mean that we excuse what happened. It certainly doesn't mean punishment for wrongdoing is not just. Consequences still occur as a result of choices. Instead, this means we can choose to give forgiveness to others because it's the free gift that we have also received. We discover a newfound sense of freedom when we forgive others who wrong us. We're no longer allowing the wrongdoing to impact us. We're showing love to others by letting go of the resentment in our hearts, which is the model set forth by Jesus Himself. As John wrote in 1 John 4:19 (NLT), "We love each other because he loved us first."

We choose to show love through forgiveness because Jesus first decided to show love to us when we didn't deserve it. When we forgive as Jesus does, we receive healing now and for eternity. We can be free of the hindrances of the past. We can be so free that we begin to pray for those who have wounded us.

Forgiveness releases us from the hold our enemies had on us. Forgiveness destroys the root of bitterness so we can live our lives in true freedom. We win the war because we fight *from* victory, not *for* victory. Jesus has already won the war and earned the victory. Our status has changed, and we live as transformed people made new by His grace.

In the ancient Garden of Eden, Satan brought this fight to humanity's doorstep. The first seeds of this battle were sown—seeds of enmity that would grow into a war waged within the human heart for our souls. God never intended for us to trade our freedom for the chains of sin. Instead, humans surrendered their position of authority and freedom from God for something of lesser value. They bought into the lie that their way would be better than God's way. We fight this same battle daily when faced with choosing our way or God's way.

Despite our tendency to choose sin and selfishness, God made a way for us to return to Him. Dutch Sheets (one of my favorite authors) once wrote, "Father, when Adam and Eve fell in the garden, You did not abandon them. Instead, You lovingly covered them, continued to provide for them, and declared – hidden in a prophetic mystery – how You would crush the serpent's newly gained headship over the human race and the earth. Calvary's explosive deliverance crushed Satan's authority over all the earth and delivered humankind from his authority. Your body, the Ekklesia [2], is now Your enforcer of this crushing blow. Obviously, we do not do so perfectly, but we are growing in our understanding of this partnership with You."

Hallelujah. What incredible news this is for each of us. I can't help but think of the words of 1 Corinthians 15:57 (NLT): "But thank God! He gives us victory over sin and death through our Lord Jesus Christ."

Foundations

My parents were God-loving, Bible-believing Christians. We would attend church at least twice each week, and some weeks, we would even go three times. They made every effort to read us the Bible and pray with us each evening. I first heard about salvation at age four and understood it as best as a four-year-old possibly could. I decided I wanted Jesus to forgive me and come and live in my heart. I prayed this prayer one Sunday morning in church as I sat on my dad's lap at our small home church.

We wouldn't stay at this church forever. Eventually, we began attending a new church in Derry, PA. While attending both there and the Christian school our church ran, I grew and matured and began to see many hypocrisies that turned me away from wanting to be a part of the church. In the introduction, I told you about my experience on my first day of first grade. I didn't tell you that this happened at this Christian school on the first day it was open. This experience filled me with

---

[2] "Ekklesia" is the Greek word used throughout the original New Testament text for the Church.

anger, as well as a sense of hatred toward school and a general distrust of all authority figures in my life.

From that moment, an inner rebellion began to brew. I longed for an existence beyond the confines of the church's walls. My goal was to escape the clutches of authority, seize control of my future, and craft my identity independent from the church. Instead of people laughing at me, I would control the narrative and have them laugh with me. At times, I would act as the class clown. I would create the laughter so it wasn't directed at my expense.

Looking back, most of my negative experiences with the abuse of authority happened in that school. The leadership was toxic, in large part due to their lack of respect for spiritual authority. I won't list all the details here, but one particular experience exemplifies the depth of my frustration. Because of a lie told by another student who happened to be the principal's nephew, I was punished. This intensified the hatred in my heart for authority and for the church. How could I ever trust these people?

I praise God for healing my heart since these experiences occurred over 37 years ago. The Lord has helped me forgive and let go of the past. The experience was challenging, but I'm thankful for the lessons learned. These events taught me that the church is led by imperfect people, which means that not all churches are governed as God intended.

Although the church intends to represent God on earth, this standard isn't always met.

I can't stress this enough: God is not synonymous with the church. God is merciful, kind, and forgiving. He calls His followers to humility and embodies it Himself by taking the form of a man and submitting to death on a cross (see Philippians 2:5-11). God does not humiliate, nor is He contradictory or hypocritical. God is good and perfect. God has great plans for all of us, despite how people may try to divert these plans through evil actions.

Unfortunately, the people who seek to cause us harm are often the same people we're told are worthy of our trust. These people are put in positions of authority and called to represent the heart and character of God. Still, they often fail because of a lack of godliness in their own lives. They are fallible people, just like all of us.

Don't allow these people to steal the plans or destroy the future God has designed for you. Refuse to let adverse circumstances dictate the direction of your life. Throughout my time in school, I unwittingly yielded control. I allowed a season of my life to be stolen because of events outside my control. These situations unknowingly planted seeds of bitterness in my heart that would later take root.

Although I asked Jesus into my heart at age four, the fire of my faith had faded from my life within a few short years due to experiences in school, church, and with my so-called "friends" down the road. I had seen the worst of what the world had to offer, and the more I experienced, the more I craved. Similarly, the more I experienced the abuse of authority, the more I resisted authority in general. I couldn't even trust positive authority figures because, to me, they belonged in the same category as the authority figures who had used their power to hurt me.

An all-out war was waging inside me. My church life and my worldly life were in constant conflict, and this spiritual battle would last for several years. Although shots had already been fired, I didn't realize at the time that the casualties had only just begun.

Chapter Three:
Paradise Lost

Before continuing my story, it's important to acknowledge that while the specifics of our struggles may differ, we're all caught in a similar fight. Whether we realize it or not, we're all fighting the same wars our ancestors have been battling for years. This tension is nothing new. The tension began thousands of years ago and continues to this day.

Some of us are aware of what's happening, but others are totally oblivious. Some people in the world believe they are living in a fairy tale. Still, some feel like collateral damage because they allow past experiences and trauma to keep them from experiencing God's promises in their lives.

However, there's also an unseen realm that's just as real as our physical world. Majestic beings created to serve God's heavenly throne exist in this space. They work on God's behalf to help carry out His plan. The primary purposes of these spiritual figures are service, worship, and battle. Although these messengers and fierce guardians have powers that go beyond our own abilities, they are like us in that they also have the ability to choose their actions.

Among all these creatures, there's one that's unlike the others. This individual was given power and authority over all the other Heavenly hosts. We learn about this unique character in passages such as Ezekiel 28:12-15 (NKJV), which reads:

"'Thus says the Lord God: 'You were the seal of perfection, Full of wisdom and perfect in beauty. You were in Eden, the garden of God; Every precious stone was your covering: The sardius, topaz, and diamond, Beryl, onyx, and jasper, Sapphire, turquoise, and emerald with gold. The workmanship of your timbrels and pipes Was prepared for you on the day you were created. You were the anointed cherub who covers; I established you; You were on the holy mountain of God; You walked back and forth in the midst of fiery stones. You were perfect in your ways from the day you were created, Till iniquity was found in you.'"

This Being was an angel (a cherub angel, to be precise). In today's world, cherubs are often depicted in paintings and cartoons as obese children with wings. I don't know who created this idea, but it's nothing like the truth. Cherubs are powerful figures who walk before God's fierce, fiery glory in Heaven. They are not fat or weak.

There are various types of spiritual beings described in Scripture, each with different ranks or duties. This particular one had jewels and instruments faceted onto his body. He had superior influence above all the armies of Heaven and was bestowed by God with extraordinary powers and abilities. God named this creature "Lucifer" and charged him with leading, directing, and carrying out God's bidding.

Unfortunately, Lucifer succumbed to a deadly force called the sin of pride that permeated his heart and mind. He experienced the pitfalls we read about in Proverbs 16:18 (NLT) ("Pride goes before destruction, and haughtiness before a fall.") and Isaiah 14:12 (NLT) ("How you are fallen from heaven, O shining star, son of the morning! You have been thrown down to the earth, you who destroyed the nations of the world.")

Where pride exists, a fall is just around the corner. As was the case when Lucifer gave into the sin of pride, these tumbles often happen from high places. Isaiah recounts this tragedy in his prophecy when he says, "For you have said in your heart: 'I will ascend into heaven, I will exalt my throne above the stars of God; I will also sit on the mount of the congregation On the farthest sides of the north; I will ascend above the heights of the clouds, I will be like the Most High.' Yet you shall be brought down to Sheol, To the lowest depths of the Pit." (Isaiah 14:13-15, NKJV)

In his pride, Lucifer thought he could be like God. His heart was hardened to the point where he thought he could overthrow the most powerful One to ever exist – the same Being who created him. This may sound crazy, but it's a precise reminder of how sin works. Sin will lie to you. Sin will deceive you. Sin comes with a substantial cost.

Consider this story from the prophetic book of Revelation:

> "And war broke out in heaven: Michael and his
> angels fought with the dragon; and the dragon
> and his angels fought, but they did not prevail,
> nor was a place found for them in heaven any

longer. So the great dragon was cast out, that serpent of old, called the Devil and Satan, who deceives the whole world; he was cast to the earth, and his angels were cast out with him. Then I heard a loud voice saying in heaven, 'Now salvation, and strength, and the kingdom of our God, and the power of His Christ have come, for the accuser of our brethren, who accused them before our God day and night, has been cast down.'"

(Revelation 12:7-10, NKJV)

Ultimately, sin and evil do not win. In Luke 10, Jesus tells His disciples about seeing Satan "fall from heaven like lightning!" (Luke 10:18, NLT). Although the consequences of sin are very real, they also don't represent the end of the story.

Paradise Paradox

We often see name changes in Scripture as a symbolic representation of an identity shift. After his rebellion, Lucifer was no longer called by his original name. Instead, he was referred to as "Satan" or "the devil." The Greek term for devil is διάβολος ('diabolos'), and it carries malicious or slanderous connotations. Similarly, the name Satan signifies a hostile opponent. Jesus speaks to these concepts in John 10:10 (NKJV), "The thief does not come except to steal, and to kill, and to destroy."

After Satan's fall, he could no longer be in God's presence because of his iniquities. Instead, he became the adversary of all that is good, holy, true, and pure. He vehemently opposes God, His Word, and His followers. His goal is to destroy the good world God created. Satan is the father of sin, and he hates everything that belongs to God. You're included in this grouping since you were created by God and formed in God's image.

The war happening in our lives exists because of Satan's presence in the world. He and his fallen angels will do everything possible to distract or derail God's plan in your life. The war that began in Heaven is now taking place on Earth. It won't last forever, but we must be aware of its impact on our everyday lives.

John reminds us of this significance in Revelation 12:12 (NKJV) when he writes, "Therefore rejoice, O heavens, and you who dwell in them! Woe to the inhabitants of the earth and the sea! For the devil has come down to you, having great wrath, because he knows that he has a short time."

Satan desires nothing more than our destruction. He dreams of annihilating all the goodness in our lives. How will we respond?

Lion's Den

August 1994 brought about the start of the new academic year. I had recently graduated from the eighth grade at our church's private school and was preparing to attend a public high school. This territory was utterly foreign, and I had no idea what was ahead.

I felt like fresh meat in a den of hungry lions. On the first day, I wore a shirt with a giant Jesus face on the front. I intended to let everyone know who I was and what I stood for. To be honest, it was a strange decision. Everyone should feel free and unafraid to live out their faith, but only when they have the necessary strength and genuine convictions. I had neither. My stance was weak, and my faith was on the rocks.

Something about wearing that shirt communicated to my new classmates that I was ready and open for a challenge. That also wasn't true. I was far from prepared for the resulting alienation. As I walked into the cafeteria for lunch, I walked past table after table that was either full or unwelcoming. I found the last empty table and sat down by myself. Eventually, two other "rejects" who couldn't find anywhere else to sit sat beside me.

My first thought was "I hate high school." My second was the same intention I had on my first day of first grade when my math teacher embarrassed me in front of the entire class: "I won't let this happen again."

The next day, I dressed like the other kids. I asked my mom to take me to the store so I could buy the same bookbag everyone else had. I was unwilling to live with rejection and ready to do whatever it took to earn acceptance and escape this undesirable situation. It certainly didn't help that I started in a new school after eight years of private school. Most of these kids had known each other since elementary and middle school.

This didn't stop me from trying to fit in. Over the next few months, I learned to talk like the other kids. I made the same jokes they did. I searched for opportunities to garner attention and prioritized getting noticed by others so that I would fit in. After six months of hard work, I was called up from the "rejects" table when another group offered to make room for me. Finally, I fit in. And I liked it.

We all want to be noticed. No one likes getting ridiculed or left out. The fear of rejection, memories of the past, and humiliating experiences lead us to do things we wouldn't otherwise do. We think we're operating in survival mode, but we're really acting from fear of others.

I don't intend to make excuses for my decisions. I said and did wrong things because I didn't care. My only desire was to survive the lion's den, but I was losing a more critical battle. I bought into Satan's lies. I began to pull away from my church and the principles of God's Word. The foundation built in my life's early days was gradually replaced by worldly desires and the lusts of the flesh.

Bad Decisions

By sophomore year, I was hanging out with a group that didn't share any of the values my family instilled in me since childhood on the farm. I was learning more than I ever could have imagined about drugs, sex, and other topics that should be out of bounds for high school students. Unfortunately, given the state of our society, these are all-too-common issues for children at this age. Many people don't prioritize boundaries anymore, and they will call you a bigot or intolerant if you try to create them.

Because I didn't have firm standards, I found too many opportunities to experiment with temptations that compromised my faith. If you knew much about the people whose homes these events were taking place in, you would be shocked. These weren't the people you would expect to host these types of gatherings. Many of them were churchgoers. Perhaps they were too naive to know what was happening, or maybe they simply didn't care.

I know this continues to happen today, often at younger ages than ever before. As the idea of boundaries becomes even more endangered, many people fail to draw the line between right and wrong. I wasn't more than twelve years old the first time I saw pornography, and I recently saw a statistic that said children today typically have their first encounter when they are five years old. This indicates that something is seriously wrong and broken in our world.

As I grew older, I had an opportunity to act on various temptations. My first encounter with drugs happened at a trusted family friend's home. This was a crucial turning point for me. From that moment on, I submitted entirely to the war in my soul. I no longer cared about the values I was taught growing up. I abandoned all the practices I had learned at home and at church. To support the bad habits that I was building, I began stealing.

I'm ashamed to tell you these things, but you must understand how far I fell from where I began. I'll spare some details because I don't want to glorify anything I did. I simply want you to understand the power of God's redemptive nature and the impact of my loving parents, who refused to let me live this way.

Chapter Four:
The Road Back

During these lost high school years, my heart grew cold. I still attended church, but only because I had no other choice. I was getting pretty skilled at pretending I was doing the right thing, and I always managed to avoid getting caught....at least for a while.

Despite what I believed then, I now recognize that many people at my church truly loved and served God. There were plenty of believers who weren't hypocrites. Being a resentful teenager, I simply lumped everyone into the same category because I was angry and stubborn.

Many people tried to get through to me because they recognized that something was spiritually wrong. I thank God for my former youth pastor at the Derry church who saw me and for all the wise women praying for me regularly, even when my heart was hard. My parents always believed the best about me and trusted me with great freedom to come and go. In their minds, I had never given them a reason not to trust me. Still, I was regularly betraying their trust and overstepping the boundaries of our home behind their backs.

I refused to let the godly love so many people showed me change my heart. I couldn't let them get a foothold because I wanted to continue living this way. I was enjoying myself and loving the acceptance of my classmates and peers. I even came to church drunk one morning because of a late night of partying after working at the local amusement park.

Throughout this season of life, God tried to get my attention in subtle and merciful ways. Every interaction with a Christian represented an opportunity to confess my sins and repent. Instead of leaning in, I ran further and faster in the opposite direction.

I can't definitively say if this was God's plan, but I know He used a pretty girl to get my attention. You might question if God works this way, but I believe God can use anything He desires to grab our focus. The summer before my junior year, I met this girl at a friend's house after a church fundraiser where she volunteered with her family. I hadn't volunteered, but I showed up afterward to hang out. I jumped at the opportunity to strike up a conversation with her as everybody else was cleaning up after the event.

We began dating shortly afterward. I thought I was in love, but our budding relationship wasn't healthy. Like me, this girl was hiding many things from her family, but I didn't see this as a red flag. I wanted to be with her, and since she was attending church, I decided to begin attending church with her (as any lovestruck teenage boy would have done).

Little did I know that God would ultimately use this relationship to bring me back to church. By this time, I had stopped attending our home church in Derry. I wanted to distance myself from this congregation as much as possible. My dad worked as a traveling salesman and was often away from home. When he was gone, I gave my mom a hard time on Sundays and Wednesdays when she tried to motivate us to attend church. She grew tired of my arguing and excuses and agreed to let me skip church at times. Throughout the week, after-school practices for various sports were my ticket to avoiding weeknight classes and Bible studies. I could have made it on time but made every effort to miss it.

I didn't want to be at any church, but I liked being with this girl, and she couldn't escape as easily as me. I decided if she had to be there, I would attend. As I spent more time at church, I connected with her youth pastor and his wife. This relationship played a significant role in showing me God's plan and purpose for me.

Although their influence doesn't show up fully until the next chapter of my story, I sincerely appreciate how they embraced me wholeheartedly despite most people's negative opinions about me. Admittedly, their dark hair quickly began to gray as they got to know me. I can take all the credit for this!

Wake Up Call

I attended a Christian Missionary Alliance (CMA) camp in Mahaffey, PA as a teenager. If you don't know, Mahaffey is near Punxsutawney, PA, where Phil the Groundhog famously resides. I've seen plenty of cousins but never Phil himself. I refuse to wait outside at 5 a.m. in the bitter winter cold to see a glorified rat.

Most of my memories at this camp have less to do with seeing groundhogs and more to do with spending time with friends, playing in volleyball and basketball tournaments, eating cheap hamburgers at the snack shack, and waiting in line for over an hour each evening after the worship service for the camp's famous milkshakes. However, there were other reasons why I went. My motives weren't entirely pure, and I did many things I shouldn't have done at this camp.

Nevertheless, I was required to attend church services daily in a building dubbed "The Tabernacle." The camp leadership worked hard to line up entertaining speakers and talented musicians, but my heart was hard. I never listened to the speakers and didn't care at all about what they had to say. I was living my life the way I wanted and had no plans to change my mind.

I remember one story from the dozens of sermons I had to sit through. It was about a football player who suffered a gruesome, career-ending injury. After a brutal hit and an awkward fall, his tibia bone was protruding from his skin. This compound fracture ended his football career. For a reason I can't explain, the story stuck with me. Still, I couldn't tell you what the message was about that morning.

After lunch, I was eager to head to the basketball court with my friends to begin a tournament we had signed up for earlier in the week. The bracket was finished, and the teams were chosen, but this was our first game. I was matched on defense against a childhood friend considerably larger than I was. At 5'8" and 165 pounds, I wasn't a pushover. However, I had my work cut out for me as I tried to keep up with my 6'2", 200-pound counterpart.

At one point during the game, I quickly pivoted to go after a loose ball. My larger friend attempted to do the same but stumbled over my left foot as I reached for the ball. The ensuing "snap" momentarily silenced the entire court, and the deafening quiet was quickly replaced by horrific screams as everyone - myself included - caught a glimpse of my leg. Similar to the football player from the story I had heard that morning, my bone was pushing against my skin.

Panicked and in shock, I vaguely remember hearing a staff member on the phone with the 911 operator. "We need an ambulance. We have a compound fracture." As a crowd gathered around me to look at what was happening, I pounded the ground and writhed. Attempts by others to console me did little to numb the intense pain.

As I watched a man walk toward me from across the camp with a black medical bag, my mind was in a fog. He only had 200 feet to go before reaching me, but it seemed he was 100 miles away. Every second seemed like an hour as I experienced pain worse than anything I could have imagined. To make matters worse, a crowd of fellow campers and staff members were surrounding me and staring at my deformed leg.

This was the first time I had ever experienced a significant fracture, and it completely changed the plans I thought I had for the upcoming summer. These were not wholesome plans. Ironically, my injury may have protected me from the self-inflicted danger and natural consequences these activities could have produced. However, as these plans evaporated in an instant, I was upset.

Laying on the court in excruciating pain, I thought the moment would never end. After what seemed like an eternity, the man was kneeling by my side. I heard the blaring siren of an ambulance in the background as he gave my leg medical attention. I closed my eyes as he grabbed my leg. There may have been a hundred people surrounding me, but they were all silent.

In an instant, something incredible happened. One moment, I'm lying on the ground with my eyes closed. Suddenly, I sat up straight. I felt no pain in my leg. I watched in amazement as this man slid his thumbs straight down my tibia bone. I thought, "My leg is straight? How is this even possible?"

In case it wasn't clear, my tibia bone, which was sticking out of my leg less than a few moments ago, was now fully straight and healed. My leg was no longer broken! The man disappeared back into the woods with his medical bag. When the paramedics arrived, they weren't quite as impressed as everyone else who had been watching these events take place. The counselor who had initially called told them they were no longer needed, and they left confused and slightly annoyed.

I met this counselor sixteen years later. I was attending a church leadership event where Pastor James Llewellyn was speaking about a youth camp at Mahaffey and a young man who was miraculously healed from a compound fracture. Stunned, I interrupted him and yelled, "That was me!"

Pastor James now serves as the Senior Pastor of the Greensburg Alliance Church in Greensburg, PA. Here's what he had to say about that day at camp:

"Early in my ministry, I was assigned to run the sports at Mahaffey camp. At that time, every licensed worker had to volunteer for at least one week of camp. Family camp was my week to serve. At that time, the basketball tournament was a big deal and was very competitive. One afternoon, a young adult team was playing a very competitive game. I was working on the bracket when I heard the screams for help.

I ran onto the court and saw Dave lying there in excruciating pain. I looked, and he had a broken leg, and it was bad. He had a compound fracture, and you could see the bone pushing against the skin.

I immediately sent for the camp director and nurse, and I had someone call 911 because we knew he needed medical attention. I was trying to get people back away from him while others were trying to comfort and keep him calm. In the middle of all this, a man came walking down. I clearly remember he had a bag and wore a dress shirt and a tie. He knelt down beside him and said, 'Let's all pray.'

As we prayed, everyone closed their eyes and held hands. When the man finished praying, we opened our eyes; Dave's leg was back together and completely healed. I mean, he was able to get up and start playing again, healed. The strangest part of the story is this is the first time anyone had ever seen the guy before or since. When the man finished praying, he simply walked away and into the woods. It is still one of the craziest experiences I have had in ministry.

Shortly after, the camp nurse and director showed up and wanted to see what was going on; just then, the ambulance pulled in, and I had to explain to them that he was healed. They were a little upset. I called the ambulance but said, 'What can I say? His leg was busted in half.'

I remember they asked, 'Which one?' I pointed to Dave, who was playing basketball, and said, 'That kid.' What an amazing experience of God's healing power."

As I look back and wonder why I was the one who experienced this incredible event, I recognize that God was using these circumstances to save me from the dark path I was headed down. God needed to get my attention, and the memory of this day is as vivid now as it was 26 years ago.

God can do anything in an instant, but life doesn't always work this way. Sometimes, we don't hear an answer to our prayers as quickly as we would like. Know that God still hears your prayers even if He doesn't instantly intervene, and don't stop reaching out to God with all your needs and wants. Believe in Him, and you will see His hand working in your life. Hear Jesus' words in Matthew 7:7-8 (NLT) as He says, "Keep on asking, and you will receive what you ask for. Keep on seeking, and you will find. Keep on knocking, and the door will be opened to you. For everyone who asks, receives. Everyone who seeks, finds. And to everyone who knocks, the door will be opened."

I'll forever be grateful for those who were praying for my soul. I'm so glad they didn't give up on me in my stubbornness. While my leg injury rattled me for a moment, it didn't stop me from the dangerous pursuit I was on. God was screaming at me, trying to get my attention, but I wasn't listening. Most people would have received the message, but not me.

What I didn't know was that something even worse than a compound fracture was just around the corner.

Tough Love

As summer drew to a close and a new school year began, the memories of my camp experience quickly faded. I was the same stubborn, hard-hearted teenager as before. One day, I lied to my parents and said I was going to a friend's house after soccer practice to work on homework. The location was important, partly because this was before cell phones, and my parents always wanted to know where I would be in case they needed to reach me.

I didn't go to this friend's house, and unless "homework" was a code word for getting high, that wasn't in my plans either. After we got "toasted," my friend George (not his real name) and I decided to get a group of guys together to go to wing night at a local bar and grill. We sat at the restaurant, and I asked for my regular order of 20 wings. Even when I wasn't high, I could eat like a horse and never gain an ounce.

When our food came out, I was just about to dig in when one of my friends asked from across the table, "David, why is your dad here?" I thought he was kidding, so I gave him a momentary glance and laughed.

"No, really, he's here," my friend said with fear in his eyes.

The hair on the back of my neck quickly shot up. My dad's deep voice reminds me of Darth Vader, and you can almost hear The Imperial March when he walks into the room. He unknowingly intimidated my friends; at that age, I was intimidated by him as well.

My dad marched toward our table. "I thought you were at your friend's house studying?" His voice carried a serious tone as it reverberated.

"Dad, I came here after we were done studying to eat with the guys," I lied.

"Let's go," he said as he grabbed the back of my shirt and pulled me to my feet, nearly causing the chair I was sitting on to fall to the ground.

"But I have to pay for my food!" I retorted.

"Your friends are paying for your food," he bellowed as he whisked me away to the parking lot. I watched the table as we left and caught every one of my friends' white, stunned faces staring back at me.

The ride home was dark and silent. "Dad, what is this all about?" I asked indignantly. He didn't respond. I was growing sick, and I quickly sobered up. At that moment, adrenaline began coursing through my body. It made me feel more alert and aware than I had felt in some time. I knew what was coming. I felt it deep in the pit of my stomach. I had been caught, and I was terrified.

When we arrived home, my dad still hadn't said a word. When we came inside, my mom and younger sister were sitting on the living room couch. Nearby on the coffee table was my stash of drugs. My mother was bawling.

"Charity, go to your room," my dad demanded to my sister.

My parents were broken, and it was not a pretty sight. I had no answers when my mom pleaded with me to tell her why. My dad wanted to know where I got the drugs. Hoping to appease the situation, I told him. My dad said he had been in his room praying when he felt God speaking to him and telling him where to look in my bedroom. When he checked that location, he found what he suspected I was hiding.

"Tonight, you're sleeping in your sister's room with the door open," my dad said. Her room was directly across from theirs. He said he wanted to make sure I wouldn't run.

This sounded strange. Why would I run, I thought? It quickly became apparent with my dad's following comment.

"Tomorrow, I'm taking you to the police station and turning you in."

I had no words. I was simply petrified of what might happen next. "You better pray that God has mercy on you," my dad admonished.

I couldn't think of the last time I had prayed, but I prayed that night. When you think you might go to jail, all bets are off.

Mercy

The next day, I walked past jail cells at the Latrobe police station until I reached an office with a single chair seated in the middle of the room. If you've ever watched a documentary called "Scared Straight," you can envision what I experienced that day.

I don't remember much, but I remember being fully compliant. I answered every question and did everything the officer asked me to do. This particular officer was an imposing figure. He was the picture of masculinity, a perfectly chiseled figure who spit in my face as he yelled (not talked).

I had enough drugs in my possession to warrant five years. I was also old enough to be tried as an adult. I didn't want to go to jail. You always think you'll be tough in situations like this, but I quickly sold out when I had a chance to save myself.

It was me or the other guy, and I threw the other guy under the bus. From that day on, I was branded a narc at high school. The police were determined to discover the source of these drugs, and I cooperated. Because of my willingness to share information and my dad's boldness to turn me in, the police trusted I was in capable hands and allowed me to go home.

I didn't have to go to jail and wasn't sent to any programs. I was dumbfounded. I knew kids who did less and still had to serve time. What was happening?!

Looking back, I believe that God showed me mercy. If charges were pressed, it would have derailed the plan God had for me later in life. I didn't know it then, but those foolish choices almost ruined the incredible future God had designed for me.

We serve a God who hears our prayers even when we're at our worst. God chooses to have mercy on us and gives us infinitely more than we deserve. I'm grateful that God knows what I need more than I do, and I don't know where I would be if God hadn't saved me from myself. I fully resonate with Paul's words from

Romans 5:6 (NLT): "When we were utterly helpless, Christ came at just the right time and died for us sinners."

God loves you too much to watch you throw your life away. I received tremendous mercy in one of my lowest moments, both from my Heavenly Father and my earthly father. It's incredible how tough love and mercy can work together to call us back to the life we were intended to live.

Redemption

That intervention was horrible and necessary; weeks later, I was still paying the price. Since that day, I was essentially on house arrest. I had no phone privileges, was suspended from the soccer team, and couldn't use my parents' cars. My girlfriend and I broke up because her parents (understandably) wanted me as far away as possible. I couldn't even pee with the door closed. All I could do was attend school, attend church, eat meals with my family, and read books.

One day, I got a call from a friend at church who I hadn't hung out with for some time. I'll call him Mark, though it's not his real name. Mark was disgusted with me because he felt I was throwing my life away. Even though I had lost my phone privileges, my parents allowed me to speak with Mark. He invited me to a small group Bible study at our former youth pastor's home in Derry. At the time, I was still going to my ex-girlfriend's church in hopes of seeing her, even though her parents wouldn't allow it.

Because I badly wanted to leave the house, I accepted his invitation. On the night I went, we were studying the book of Philippians. Unlike my days at summer camp, I listened intently to the pastor's words. I was captivated by what he had to say about God's love for us.

That evening, I took the study book home and continued reading. I was on one couch in our living room, and my dad was sitting on the opposite couch. We still hadn't talked much since the incident a few weeks back, so I was surprised when he began to speak.

"David, I've been praying for you, and I know about the books under your bed." He was referring to my stack of witchcraft books. As I mentioned before, my path was getting pretty dark. "God spoke to me and told me that if something doesn't change in your heart and you die today, you're going to Hell."

I felt like a lightning bolt had just hit my chest. It was as if the couch had disappeared beneath me, and I could look straight down into the pit of Hell. It was a strange sensation, but it felt terrifyingly real. Words can't fully describe what I experienced in that moment.

As shocked as I was, I tried to remain calm. I slowly stood up, walked to my bedroom, and fell on my knees beside my bed. I began to sob uncontrollably, pouring my heart out to God and begging for forgiveness.

This was the night I gave my heart back to Jesus as a 17-year-old. I started reading my Bible on my own to learn what I had been missing all along, and it transformed me. Verses like Romans 6:23 (NLT), which says, "For the wages of sin is death, but the free gift of God is eternal life through Christ Jesus our Lord," replaced the evil, self-sabotaging beliefs I had carried throughout my teenage years.

I wasn't afraid of going to Hell anymore. I no longer felt pain, disappointment, shame, and embarrassment for what I had done, even though I lived in a small town where everyone knew what had happened. The emptiness in my heart disappeared, filled with the presence of a loving God who had been pursuing me all along – even when I didn't recognize it.

As I laid my face on the bed, the weight of God's mercy settled on me. I made it back to Him. I made it back to where I belonged. I was home. I was the lost sinner James spoke about when he wrote, "you can be sure that whoever brings the sinner back from wandering will save that person from death and bring about the forgiveness of many sins." (James 5:20, NLT)

That night was one of the best nights of my life. It was the night that I truly learned what it means to receive God's free gift of the forgiveness of sins, made possible by the sacrifice of His Son, Jesus Christ.

Chapter Five:
Runaway Purpose

Sometimes, you don't know your direction in life, and that's okay. You don't always have to have it all figured out. The worst thing you can do is give up and stop moving. You can't steer a stagnant ship, and what good is a vessel if it doesn't take you anywhere?

Life cannot be an unplanned adventure. It's careless, dangerous, wasteful, and hurts the ones you love the most. I had to learn how to chart a course instead of driving aimlessly.

I may not have had it all together. I may have not had a five-year plan. However, one thing I did have was a passion for something greater in life, and I was willing to follow that desire to discover more. I was born for something more than what I was experiencing, and I was determined to find it! I did not realize then that the "now" we experience is necessary to prepare us for "more" later. I had to learn this the hard way.

Each one of us has an innate desire and longing for the possibilities of what could be in life. We are born with a passion for something more and a desire to leave a lasting legacy. We want to know that our lives count for something. Ecclesiastes 3:11 (NLT) says, "He has planted eternity in the human heart." This innate desire for something greater drove my early journey to discover God's purpose and plan for my life.

God bless Pastor Carl and Norma Emerick's souls and ministries. They were responsible for helping me realize that God could still use me for His plans even though I was still a mess. They helped me see that God wasn't through with me yet.

Returning to God didn't transform me into a perfect, well-behaved teenager overnight. I was committed to attending church and eager to demonstrate that I had grown and become a better person. I wanted everyone to notice this transformation, primarily because it would pave the way for me to spend time with the girl I wasn't allowed to see.

One night, I volunteered to help with a kids' ministry event. I had only been attending church again for two weeks after the incident involving my dad and the police. While I genuinely wanted to serve and make the right choices, my selfish desires persisted simultaneously, and the girl's parents weren't fooled.

A heart change doesn't mean we have it all figured out. We still have to grow in our faith and mature. My learning curve was steeper than some of the other teenagers who were present. As I think back on my gradual transformation, the words of 2 Corinthians 3:18 (NLT) come to mind: "So all of us who have had that veil removed can see and reflect the glory of the Lord. And the Lord—who is the Spirit—makes us more and more like him as we are changed into his glorious image."

I was changing and growing in my faith. I was learning how to become more like God and to do the things that would cause me to find the best success and fulfillment in life. I was learning to serve. Carl and Norma loved me unconditionally and saw tremendous potential in me, even though they hardly knew me. I was an obnoxious, energetic, dream-filled young man, and they recognized God was leading me to them, and I needed their help. I never returned to my parent's church, but they were happy I was going somewhere.

Despite the underlying wrong motives for attending, I was at least showing up. I heard the Word of God preached, unlike I had ever heard it before. Carl and the church's senior pastor both had a gift from the Lord to share timeless truths from the Bible that resonated deeply with me. All of a sudden, these principles started making sense. I was hearing the truth in a way that I could understand. I wanted more! Unlike last time, I was listening, and it made all the difference.

The more I heard, the more I began to apply Biblical truths to my life in simple, practical ways. The more I used these truths, the more they worked! This stuff was real, and I wanted more. I started to love attending church. Throughout the rest of my junior year, people began to see a change in my life. I was no longer the same person. I was different. I was the living embodiment of the person Paul describes in 2 Corinthians 5:17 (NLT).

> *"This means that anyone who belongs to Christ has become a new person. The old life is gone; a new life has begun!"*

I loved this new life I was discovering. I had no idea what I was doing, but I wanted to be close to where all the action was taking place. During the next two summers, I spent nearly every day at the church. After work or summer sports practices, I would sit in the secretary's office.

I can imagine what each of the church's staff members thought as they saw me, but I don't want to articulate them. They didn't know what to do with me the first few days. To be fair, I didn't know what to do with myself, either. That's why I was there. I was bursting at the seams. I wanted to learn. I wanted to do something!

As I came back day after day, a routine began to form. Norma, the church secretary, would ask how my day was. She started having me help with projects around the church. I was so thankful and eager to do each one. Since I was volunteering now, I was often invited to have lunch with the team of Norma, Pastor Warner, and his wife, who was his personal secretary. Pastor Carl could only join us occasionally since he had a full-time job at the local hospital. This team of God-loving people poured into me. They shared stories with me of the miraculous, simple principles from the Bible and challenged me to believe in God for the best in my life. I loved every minute of it.

I also contributed. I worked at Red Lobster and shared my 50% discount with everyone. It was a small price to pay in return for the invaluable moments I would get for the next two years.

These benefits went far beyond free lunches. I eventually served as a youth leader in the youth group, and Carl and Norma continued to invest in my life. They included me in dinners at their house, dinners out at restaurants, and occasional trips to do ministry projects. Carl was available for me at all hours of the day. I had this newfound hunger for more of God's plan for my life, but I still didn't know what to do with it. I learned how to memorize scriptures from Carl's sermons using little 4x8 notecards.

When I struggled with self-doubt and temptations late at night, Carl was there. He would meet me at Denny's for midnight meals and to pray with me. He taught me how to get alone with God and have one-on-one appointments with Him. He taught me how to cry to God for healing and put the broken pieces back together inside me.

I was so hungry for God's plan, but I had no idea what it was. By then, I had graduated high school and attended LaRoche College in Pittsburgh. I was playing college soccer and going to school to study graphic design. I didn't want to go to school for graphic design, but I was good at art, so I decided to make a career out of it. This pursuit only lasted one semester.

I left LaRoche College and came home to attend community college. I was now going to school for nursing, even though I wasn't particularly interested in being a nurse. I was also jumping from job to job.

Norma taught me many things in that church office. She would often say, "Don't despise small beginnings." This simple encouragement would change the course of my life.

Tennessee Adventure

A tiny acorn eventually turns into a mighty oak, but it doesn't happen overnight. It takes years of patience and a consistent supply of the right ingredients (water, nutrients, and sunlight) to produce growth before getting to that place of prominence.

Jesus taught us that faith works similarly in Mark 4:30-32 (NLT). He says, "How can I describe the Kingdom of God? What story should I use to illustrate it? It is like a mustard seed planted in the ground. It is the smallest of all seeds, but it becomes the largest of all garden plants; it grows long branches, and birds can make nests in its shade."

Big things start small, and it takes time for them to become what they are meant to be. If they are going to produce the right results, they must be fed consistently with the essential components. The same is true for our lives. At this point in my life, I did not have much patience. Hence, Norma tried to teach me this lesson. I would ultimately learn it, but I made it much more complicated than it had to be.

I was 18 years old. I had jumped jobs several times. I was in the middle of my first of many degree changes in college. I remember feeling so frustrated and not knowing where to unleash the dreams that were welling up inside me to do something more. I remember vividly a very pointed conversation with Norma that would stick with me for the rest of my adult life.

I had stopped at the church again on my way home from classes. To an 18-year-old constantly "starving" young man, that was like my daily Thanksgiving feast!

Being 18 and involved in college sports dangerously stretched my parents' grocery budget.

Norma often ordered Gino's Pizza, one of my favorite regular lunches back in the day, and it remains my second favorite pizza in the world. Norma was a little Mexican lady from Brownsville, TX, and she introduced me to many amazing new flavor combinations. Norma taught me to order the pizza with banana peppers. She also introduced me to authentic mole, which sparked my love for Mexican food. If the saying "you are what you eat" is true, I am Mexican, thanks to Norma! [3]

One day, we took a lunch break even though we still had work we needed to do. Norma looked at me and realized I needed help. She saw a young man with passion and determination who desperately needed to take the ship's helm and stop blowing in every direction with the wind. When she said to me, "David, don't despise small beginnings," I heard: "Stop running all over the place trying to figure it out. Buckle down where you find yourself and do the best with what you've been given." She then elaborated, "Work hard right where you're at, and God will bless you with more if you can be trusted with the little you have now. Work hard, do your best, and when the time is right, the doors will open for you."

Those words were fresh life to my weary and wandering heart. Oh, how I regret not heeding these words! I heard what she was saying, but I failed to listen genuinely. I knew what the right course of action was. God had spoken to my heart, urging me to complete

---

[3] I guess this also makes me part chicken, especially given my current day job.

one more semester at LaRoche College and finish my freshman year. I should have followed that divine guidance and stayed to finish strong. I should have remained on my college soccer team and retained my job at the Baby Gap. Yes, I said Baby Gap. Don't judge! They were hiring at the nearby mall, and I needed the income.

Feeling anxious led me to make the wrong decision. I should have taken Norma's counsel to heart. Typically, my routine was to take the one hour and twenty minutes drive home from north Pittsburgh to stay at my parents' house over the weekend. I came home late one night while I was stewing and wrestling. I was thinking about how I needed to start my future. I couldn't wait for it any longer. I didn't want to be patient anymore. I had decided to push through two more weeks, and those two weeks were over. What did Norma know anyway? If you were going to do something, you couldn't wait. You had to make it happen!

The semester was about to be over, and winter break was near. If I was going to do something, it had to be now! I talked with a friend late that night and told them, "I'm ready. I need to leave." After I hung up the phone that night at 11 p.m., I began driving, trying to figure out what to do. I stopped at a gas station to fill my car. I saw a US roadmap in a rack of AAA atlases. Remember that GPS wasn't a thing yet, and cell phones had only recently begun gaining traction.

I bought the map and filled up the gas tank. While there, I began leafing through the atlas and landed on Franklin, Tennessee. I decided I knew what I should do. I took a quick trip back home to the basement, where I essentially had my own apartment. My dad had taken over my former bedroom as his office, and a separate basement entrance allowed me to come and go as I pleased.

While my parents and sister were sleeping, I began packing my car with clothes (no suitcase), artwork in my portfolio, and a giant plastic Coke bottle piggy bank of money. At midnight, I quietly exited the driveway to begin my new adventure. And boy, was it an adventure!

Franklin, TN, is a suburb located just south of Nashville, where I thought I would realize my dreams. The trip began in midnight darkness and ended in the darkness of the wee hours of the morning. It's a good representation of my subpar choice to take the trip in the first place. It wasn't only physically dark - it was an equally dark time of indecisiveness in my life that could've ended badly.

When you walk in ignorance, making decisions based on your feelings and refusing to seek counsel from people with wisdom and experience, your journey will be shrouded in darkness and danger. This is the danger of hiding yourself in the dark and not sharing what's going on internally with someone.

Despite what so-called "experts" may tell you, you are not your own best teacher. Can you learn from the consequences of the decisions you make? Absolutely! At the same time, you'll avoid the negative consequences if you don't make the wrong decision in the first place. This is precisely what happened to me. My pastor always told me, "It's better to learn from someone else's mistakes than your own." After this wayward trip to Franklin, I learned this lesson loud and clear. Oh, how I wish I would've learned from someone else's mistake!

I might've found a better route had GPS been easily accessible then. Remember, most people weren't using cell phones yet. I simply drew a straight line on the map from Latrobe, PA, to Franklin, TN. That had to be the quickest way, right? Everyone knows that the shortest distance between two points is a straight line. In the dark, I was off for a destination I was sure would have all the answers when I arrived.

What made me choose Franklin, TN, of all places? It may sound humorous, but I had this dream in 1990 when I was ten. Perhaps you've heard of the band DC Talk, led by Toby McKeehan (better known today as TobyMac). When I heard DC Talk's music for the first time, it engaged my soul and opened up my creativity and imagination in a way I had never experienced before in my ten-year-old life.

The first CD I ever purchased was a DC Talk album. I received a portable CD player for Christmas to replace my worn-out Walkman. The album "NU Thang" had just been released. Remember, this was the 90s, and people still bought CDs when new albums came out. I was one of the first in line to purchase it and played it on repeat for the entire year. No joke. I didn't know you could wear out CDs, but the reflective silver stuff on the plastic disc can come off.

I eagerly wanted to meet these guys and was determined to find a way to work with them. Remember how I was an artist? I thought, "I could create artwork for their promotions, CD covers, T-shirt designs, you name it!" I started drawing furiously.

A couple of years later, I was old enough to join the youth group at our church, and we went on many fun adventures together. We took one particular trip to "Agape Farms" in Mt. Union, PA (about 80 miles east of Latrobe) to attend the "Creation Festival."

DC Talk was playing at the festival that year, and I wanted to meet them and give my pitch. I had been working on a sketch all year to present to them, with the plan to ask if they would hire me as an artist. The week of the festival was upon us. We pitched our tents, and each night, we lined up after the headliner to get autographs.

The night of their performance came. After they finished playing, I waited in the autograph line to meet Kevin, Michael, and everyone's favorite, Toby. The thing is, I had left my artwork at home. I was too afraid they wouldn't like it.

Instead, I reached the front and asked for their autographs. In my squeaky 12-year-old, half-man voice, I asked Michael, "Do you ever consider hiring artists to do artwork for your promotions and stuff?" He engaged me and said, "Yeah, man! Why? Are you an artist?"

I was ecstatic. I quickly replied, "YES!"

"Come here a second," Michael said. He pulled me aside and wrote down his number on a piece of paper at the ForeFront Records office. He graciously said, "Call me and send something so we can look at your work and consider it." My feet didn't touch the ground the whole way back to the campsite, and no one in our group believed what had happened! Nothing was guaranteed yet, but I felt my entire life had just changed!

In the months after "Creation Festival" that summer, I called the number Michael gave me nearly a dozen times, but I always chickened out whenever someone answered. I made up stories of why I was calling. I replied, "Wrong number," asked about hiring, and sometimes just hung up. Now, six years later, an old dream had returned in the late hours of the night. When I couldn't find a new plan, I resorted to an old one.

I felt desperate. "Let's do this once and for all," I thought. I was driving my dad's old Toyota Camry, with over 200,000 miles on it, through the hills of Kentucky when the first light began to dawn. I had already been awake for 24 hours at this point. I was tired but remained undaunted in my excitement for what I was doing and what lay ahead.

I was running on pure adrenaline, and when that began to subside, I refueled with a two-liter of Mountain Dew. Things are bound to get a little weird when you're in the middle of a 600-plus-mile trip through the hills of West Virginia, Kentucky, and Tennessee – especially as a sleep-deprived college student with questionable habits. At one point, I even thought I saw dinosaurs in the rock faces as I drove past.

Thankfully, I had the "guts" (or stupidity) to keep going and shake off the setbacks. Less "brave" (or stubborn) people would have pulled off the road and napped, but I had a destination, and nothing would stop me. I took a few stops to fill up on gas and "Dew" in some scary towns throughout Kentucky. These are the towns you've only seen in horror movies or thrillers. Yes, they exist, but I wouldn't let them deter me from my goal.

A journey that shouldn't have taken more than 10 hours lasted at least 13, possibly because I had never navigated a trip alone. I used the ruler method on the map, and it was just one poor decision in a succession of bad decisions that night. I quickly learned that you must travel slower on the minor roads that run by steep drop-offs, especially when there are no guard rails and you see signs that say "danger: explosives being used." Yeah, that's real! I'd be lying if I said I wasn't scared, especially after driving by miles of shacks considered homes built under bridges.

Finally, I reached Nashville. I was close! I decided it would be a good idea to call someone to let them know where I was. By now, it was around lunchtime.

I pulled off at the first payphone I saw. Thankfully, I had an entire Coke bottle bank full of coins (at least it was a quarter full). I knew the friend I was talking to the night before would be at school, so I called the school directly.

They answered the phone in the secretary's office, and with great excitement, I told them where I was and what I was doing. They didn't seem quite as excited as I was for some reason. I told them my plan and promised to contact them later once I figured things out.

When I hung up the phone, I had no idea a firestorm would ensue. My friend thought letting some people know what was happening would be good. I can't imagine why. By "some people," I mean everyone. This friend told my parents, Carl (my youth pastor), and his wife, and everyone we knew.

I was only 30 minutes away from Franklin. I looked up ForeFront Records in the phone book to find out how to get to my next destination. Soon after, I arrived at an underwhelming building. Obviously, this was a rented space for an operation much smaller than I had imagined. ForeFront was a fraction of the EMI Records conglomerate (now called Capitol Music Group). In my mind, I had pictured a colossal building to house the enormous musicians and stars represented by this group.

My eyes were opened to how things worked in the music industry that day. I talked to the receptionist and told her why I was there. Someone from the offices above came down to meet me. I shared my pitch and desire to design album covers, promotions, and other artistic projects. He asked if I had a resume. I wasn't prepared for him to ask that question. First missed opportunity.

Nevertheless, he took me on an impromptu 30-minute tour of the entire building. I was overjoyed. I saw the design room, an operation of one graphic designer sitting behind a computer surrounded by cool covers and original designs on the walls. "Yikes, it doesn't seem like they hire many graphic artists," I thought. Therein lies my second missed opportunity. I could have asked in advance if they were hiring and what they were looking for, but I didn't.

We continued the tour. I saw many neat things they were working on, and my guide was super friendly and hospitable. I think he saw an 18-year-old kid that was lost and searching. By the end, I was loaded with swag and free CDs. He even offered me lunch. I declined because I realized this wasn't a job interview but a courtesy to a kid someone felt bad for. I was heartbroken and just wanted to leave and return home.

I felt so dumb. My host quickly followed me to the car after I thanked him for his time. He saw my artwork in the back seat with many clothes and deduced what was happening. He said my work looked cool, but they weren't hiring graphic artists. He almost pleaded with me to stay the night on the couch. Out of more foolishness and emotion, I turned him down and immediately drove back to Pennsylvania.

Someone once told me that if you go three days without sleeping, you are considered legally insane. I don't know about those facts, but if they were true, they would explain many things about my life after this point. I wasn't able to reason by now. I was not thinking clearly at all. On the journey back through West Virginia, I brilliantly thought, "Maybe I should call someone."

I called my mom, who was very upset and concerned but surprisingly not mad. I called my youth pastor and his wife and discovered that many people were praying for me. They prayed for my safety. I felt loved by a lot of people that day.

Miraculously, I made it into my driveway at about 4 a.m. I know God was answering prayers and watching over me because I didn't remember the last 30 minutes of the trip. My brain had shut down from sheer exhaustion due to being awake almost three days straight. The last thing I remembered was parking the car.

My mom wanted to talk to me immediately, but I was "out" once my head hit the pillow. I came to consciousness again and had already begun to prepare mentally for the coming punishment. My dad had just returned home from a business trip. I heard him walking down the stairs, and my heart raced as the familiar creak of each step brought him closer to the basement. There were only about 12 steps, but it seemed like an eternity before he reached the bottom.

What I experienced that day was far different than what I expected. There was love, grace, forgiveness, and great mercy once again. My dad wrote me a letter, which we often found was an easier way for us to communicate during the tumultuous days of my young adulthood. One particular sentence jumped off the page: "David, you could've just asked for help, and your mom and I would've helped you get there."

"What?! Someone could've helped me?" This thought was the most foreign concept to hit my underdeveloped brain. Why had I not thought of that before?!

This lesson stood out far above all the many truths and principles I discovered on this wayward trip. I could have reached out to someone wiser who had lived life and made mistakes on their own, and they likely would have had something to offer me. My dad was a traveling salesman. If nothing else, he could have helped me navigate the trip.

People are always around us, but we are so closed off that we never dare ask or think someone could help. It's, in fact, the best thing we could ever do. Don't be afraid to ask for help. Solomon says it better than I could in Proverbs 15:22 (NLT): "Plans go wrong for lack of advice; many advisors bring success."

This verse is a significant truth I learned that day and every day since. You can't (and shouldn't) try to do things on your own. We all need others. Success comes through MANY advisors. Seek counsel, seek wisdom, and lean on those you can trust who have been there before. This misguided trip began and ended in darkness, but I learned it couldn't stay this way forever. And thankfully, it didn't. Eventually, I got help from those who cared for me. The light would arrive at dawn again.

Perhaps you are experiencing dark times like my Tennessee trip. You may feel like there's no way into the light or the darkness won't let up. It's not true. Dawn always comes after dark. There's hope. There are people around you who care, and if you're willing to share the secrets that are going through your heart and mind, you'll quickly learn that you're not alone.

Know who you can trust. Go to those trusted individuals and share your innermost thoughts and feelings. If you do, you'll find you never could do it yourself in the first place, and that success is waiting when you bring others into the equation.

Chapter Six: Keep Going

My first college semester ended, and the Tennessee disaster was behind me. In the second semester of my freshman year at the Community College, I was going through the motions of what I thought I should do. The gnawing desire to discover God's purpose for me was still there, and nothing seemed to satisfy me.

That same year, I attended an "Acquire the Fire" conference produced by a Christian group called Teen Mania Ministries. They aimed to create an event for young people to get excited about serving God and help them discover God's plans. I had already been on one mission trip with this group to Monterrey, Mexico, a year earlier. This time, I would answer the call to attend their year-long gap program called The Honor Academy in Garden Valley, Texas.

This place served as an internship program designed for young individuals to engage in various on-campus roles, all aimed at assisting missionaries on a global scale. The creators of The Honor Academy program envisioned it as a college campus, complete with training and Bible classes. Its purpose was to allow students to pause their regular lives and earnestly seek God while gaining clarity and direction. This concept resonated with me. I had already spent time, money, and college credits on pursuits that had little meaning, and I desperately needed greater guidance.

Through hard work, saving money, and receiving monthly support from my parents and church, I raised the necessary funds to embark on my journey to The Honor Academy in Texas. I booked a two-day Greyhound bus expedition that transported me to Garden Valley. With nothing more than a suitcase, my trusty guitar in hand, and the clothes on my back, I disembarked, feeling wholly disoriented in this quaint little town.

I must have looked lost as I scanned my surroundings for my designated ride, which was nowhere to be found. The first person I approached kindly extended an offer of work and a place to stay. I chuckled to myself because, under different circumstances, I might have taken them up on the offer. However, I had a clear destination in mind this time.

Unable to reach my campus ride, I decided to try my luck hitchhiking down a remote back road. In the scorching August heat, I was immensely relieved when a Texas-sized Ford pickup truck pulled over to the side. I eagerly hopped into the bed and loaded my belongings with the driver's assistance. Within a few minutes, we arrived at a stunningly landscaped oasis nestled amidst the wilderness of the Lone Star state.

It was August 1999. I was embarking on a journey towards something better and bigger, filled with hope that I would find all the answers I was seeking. With every interaction, class, and friendship I made, I felt one step closer to finding my path. These feelings of certainty lasted three months before the initial excitement waned. Unfortunately, I still didn't know what I wanted to do with my life. Yet, I was determined to make the most of this opportunity, to keep moving forward.

Reflecting on my journey, I understand now that this place was never guaranteed to provide all the answers to my calling. However, it did assure me that if I approached it with an open and expectant heart, I would encounter the One who possessed all the answers. The path was undoubtedly challenging. In those moments, I found solace in the wisdom shared by my youth pastor's wife: "Don't despise small beginnings." I was going to make the most of this opportunity.

I had this gift of being away from everything familiar to grow deeper in my relationship with God. It wasn't any easier, but I was in a better head space to face the challenge. This program provided many opportunities, but it was up to me to pursue what awaited me next.

Keep Moving

"But I discipline my body and bring it into subjection, lest, when I have preached to others, I myself should become disqualified." 1 Corinthians 9:27, NKJV

We would half-heartedly repeat this verse every lap around the trail. It was pitch black, cold, and sometimes raining. I didn't want to be elevating my heart rate this early.

It was time to exercise each morning at 5:00 a.m. and run our mile. I hated it. At 19 years old, I wanted to sleep more than exercise. Even now, I'm not particularly eager to exercise that early in the morning. Naturally, I am a night person. My mind becomes alert and awake when evening rolls around, and I do my best thinking. Still, I knew this exercise was essential to prepare for what was coming, so I had to get up and get moving.

Not only was it required in this internship, but I wanted to be able to climb that 14,115 foot mountain in one day. The experience of a lifetime was only a few months away, and I needed to get in shape to perform this feat. The air was thin up there. I had to build my cardiovascular health and stamina to accomplish the challenge.

The interns loaded into the buses, and we began our journey to Colorado Springs, Colorado. We arrived at the YMCA camp in the Rockies, just a short drive from Pike's Peak. Here, we'd spend a day acclimating to the thinner air. It was a much different feeling to hike around with less oxygen than on the trails in Texas. I was even more thankful I pushed myself to build lung capacity each morning up to this point.

Climb day finally arrived. We began the hike before sun up. We watched the sunrise at the mountain's base as we paced ourselves at a pretty good clip to get halfway by lunchtime. A few hours after our ascent, it was time for our PB&Js and lots of water. We made it to the midway stop. Everyone was shuffling in. A few hundred of us congregated. We had about twenty minutes to rest and gear back up with our daypacks to finish the rest of the journey. As I looked to the top of the mountain, the hike was about to get more complicated. The terrain was quickly changing.

Before we proceeded any further, the group leaders were placed into groups of five or six to ensure accountability if something went wrong. We could help if there was an injury, provide first aid, and rely on one another for encouragement. Not all of us were equal in conditioning. Some had injuries and conditions, and others were in better shape. At the beginning of our hike, the trees were tall, and the forest was thick. A few hours in, the trees began to thin out, the expanses became more extensive, and the terrain much steeper. The group started to thin out as well with the thinning forest. The air was much thinner, too, and each step became more labored. Soon, we began passing groups that were sitting down. Some had to turn back because of complications.

"Keep moving." This phrase became our motto. When certain sections of the climb became steeper with the loose ground on the trail or the hikers couldn't breathe, they would want to sit and catch their breath. We would allow them to stop briefly and get some water, but sitting down was never allowed. We saw some that couldn't bring themselves to get back up. The only option was to keep moving.

After several hours, we finally arrived at the start of the switchbacks and could see the snow-covered mountain peak. Our finish line was a little further ahead. The most challenging part of the climb was before us. Our breathing was heavy and labored, and baby steps were the name of the game. I could see before us there was one lone climber. He was a little overweight, and his group had pulled ahead of him because he couldn't keep going.

We asked amongst ourselves, "What do we do?" This poor guy couldn't go on, and we couldn't leave him alone. Mentally, he was done with this climb. His body wouldn't move, and he wanted to turn back. At this point, it meant being stuck in the dark on a mountain in Colorado with wildlife and no survival gear or food.

It was getting colder as we approached the top. We were now in the late afternoon, about 1,000 feet from the peak's summit. We were so close to our destination! Months of preparation led to this moment, and now, in the middle of the trail, we weren't moving. Our fellow intern said he couldn't take another step. He was spent, incoherent, taking shallow breaths, and very lethargic. "What do I do?" I thought to myself.

I'll be honest. The temptation was right at the top of my mind to allow the lone trekker's group to deal with him and keep moving with my group. I discovered I wasn't the only one thinking this. His group had already moved on and left him behind. I knew I couldn't leave him, so I asked questions to assess the situation. We kept to the side as best as possible to let the other hikers go around. This trail was getting dangerous, especially as it became increasingly crowded and steeper on one side of the route. We were on the last stretch to reach the top and had to figure out a solution fast.

The funny thing is, I had no idea what I was doing. I wasn't an expert hiker. I wasn't even an official leader at this point. I was a new intern hoping to have this incredible mountain-top experience. I didn't even know anyone in my current group. How did I get myself into this situation? One thing I've learned early on because of moments like this is that you don't always get to choose the moments that define you. Many times, the moment chooses you. Depending on what you do, they could change the trajectory of your life and others for the better or worse. Will you recognize the moment when it comes?

I could've chosen to ignore the person right in front of me. Instead, something rose inside, and I said, "Let's do this!" The last thing I had in my sack was a pack of jelly from our PB&J break. He needed sugar in his system. I said, "Eat this as we start taking a few steps at a time. It will give you energy, and I will have my hand on your back." He fought me for a minute, saying he just wanted us to leave him be. I said, "No, you've come too far and are making it to the top! Let's go!" The words of Paul in Galatians 6:2 (NKJV) flood my mind as I recount this story: "Bear one another's burdens, and so fulfill the law of Christ."

This guy wasn't my responsibility. Or was he? I didn't know him well, but I had seen him around campus. The fact is, this moment in time was presented to me. Maybe he wasn't my responsibility according to worldly standards, but I couldn't choose to ignore him. This guy was my age, and he needed help and encouragement. I had no desire to lift someone else's burden on this trip, but here I was, pushing someone to their destination.

We often become narrow-minded in life. We get tunnel vision regarding our daily routines. We forget that we are not islands. God put us here to make a difference and help others on their journey. I could've passed by like many others, and my celebration at the top would've been short-lived. I wouldn't have had any reward besides my own. Instead, I gave my strength to someone else who had none, and now, as we neared the last few feet of the trail, I witnessed a miraculous event.

Jimmy (not his real name) looked up and saw the finish line. Something supernatural took over his body. With tears and resolve in his eyes, strength filled his body to run. When he reached the top, he jumped up and down, declaring, "I've never done anything like this in my life! I never thought I could do this! My mom is never going to believe this." He hugged me, and we celebrated as others began high-fiving and congratulating him.

That afternoon, he recounted through pictures and the telling of the story of his fantastic accomplishment. I didn't receive any accolades from anyone, nor was I looking for any. One thing, however, did happen. My trip to the top became much more rewarding as I saw someone do something impossible. He was overweight and asthmatic. He was not in good shape. I don't think he ever was, according to his admission. Despite his efforts on the trail months before in preparation, something remarkable occurred that day. Someone believed in God for bigger things than they ever thought possible. And it happened!

We all face insurmountable objects or situations in front of us occasionally. When this happens, we tend to freeze. Sometimes, you think, "This isn't worth it," and you want to turn back. Please, I beg you, KEEP MOVING. If you can, ask for help. We have people all around us, just as in this story. Many pass us by, consumed with their desires and oblivious to the needs of those before them. Find the one who sees you. They may be people you know or strangers but have a reputation for helping. Reach out to them. Sometimes, all we need is a hand on our back and someone to tell us, "Let's go! Keep moving."

You may be passing others by on your way to your destination. Look around and see who needs you. It gets very lonely when you get to the top and have no one with you to celebrate. You may have achieved all you have set out to do, but with no one to congratulate you, high-five you, hug you, and cry tears of joy, what's the point? This life is so much better when you have someone by your side who has shared the journey with you. If you don't have anyone, find someone. Keep your eyes open and look for the opportunity. It may initially seem like a burden, but it is your moment. By doing so, you help that individual go further than they ever thought possible, and you find joy in knowing you helped them get there! Remember the words Jesus shared in Luke 6:31 (NKJV): "And just as you want men to do to you, you also do to them likewise."

Just as my time at The Honor Academy was ending, I became acutely aware of the lesson I just learned above. I was lonely. I wanted to find someone who could walk life's journey alongside me. Before I left to return home to Pennsylvania, I remember praying: "Lord, help me find the girl you have for me."

College Ministry

I barely survived, making it one month at a time on the meager finances I raised to live there in Garden Valley, TX. Thankfully, my parents found a deal and helped me get a plane ticket home so I could be with them for Christmas.

While I was home, my childhood friends started attending a college ministry group led by two girls, Sara and Melissa. They had a desire to create a place where young adults could gather together with like-minded Christians and pursue seeking God's best for their lives. It was a remarkable and unique time when most Gen Xers drifted and did not know what to do. They created an environment where we could discover God's plan for our lives together.

The first night I attended, I was amazed to see 40 or 50 young people crammed into Melissa's tiny living room, all worshiping God, eager and ready to hear a teaching from God's word by one of their peers.

I felt somewhat jealous, as though I was missing out. I went halfway across the country to pursue this, which was happening in my backyard. My internal frustrations emerged when we broke into smaller groups to pray and to discuss what we had just heard.

As we went around the room, each of us sharing, I foolishly declared, "I don't like coming home to see all these new people making friends with my friends." I had FOMO (Fear Of Missing Out). "It was okay to feel it, but keep it to yourself, David!" is what I should've told myself. I needed help adjusting to real life.

Little did I know someone was sitting in the room that night who would later be the most significant person to ever walk into my life from that moment on. This person would forever change the trajectory of my future. This person was someone I had been praying for but had yet to meet face to face. She was not thrilled or impressed with my words or arrogance that emanated and stunk up the room that evening. We wouldn't officially meet until the following spring, in April of 2000, when I came home from the internship for good.

The Potter's House

In the spring of 2000, I was back in good 'ole Latrobe, Pennsylvania. I returned with a passion for doing something impactful and significant. I had no idea what that would look like, but I hoped it would make a positive difference on this planet.

I moved into an apartment with four of my closest friends in Greensburg, 10 miles west of Latrobe. This town was the same place where we were all attending the college ministry group. I went to school during the day and worked as a pizza delivery driver at night and on weekends. Big things were happening! I say this facetiously, but I was making money. At least, I was most of the time when I wasn't being threatened at gunpoint or getting hit by drunk drivers. These are true stories, but I'll save them for another time. Regardless, I was beginning my adult years and was happy about that.

One of the college group leaders, Melissa, wanted to open a coffee house that would double as a place to share the message of Jesus. One night, I heard the more extensive pitch and immediately latched onto the idea. I was attending school to finish my business degree. The pursuit of business awakened something, and opening this coffee house gave me a focus and a purpose I could latch onto.

Even as early as ten years old, I had side hustles at school, making and selling products to other kids. Business and entrepreneurship had always been there. My parents had also always been entrepreneurs with side hustles that I would occasionally help them with. I gained an appreciation for this kind of work from them at a young age. Others also apparently saw my penchant for business. One adult approached me at church and said, "David, I think you should consider pursuing a business degree." So I did.

Over the next couple of years, I had the opportunity to apply what I had learned about business to the present project of opening a coffee house that would be about more than just selling coffee. The name would be "The Potter's House," Inspired by Jeremiah 18:2 in the NIV, "'Go down to the potter's house, and there I will give you my message.'"

We developed a business plan and designed a campaign to pitch to investors. At the first dinner we hosted, we met a family who were more interested in us who were pursuing this business than the coffee house itself. They saw a passionate group that wanted to do something big, and they wanted to help us. Over a year, they invited us to their house and farm to spend time mentoring us in business.

They were qualified, too. Their family owned a large Christian book publishing company and distributor.

They had the chops, and we had a front-row seat. We learned so much during this time. Sadly, nothing ever came to fruition. The furthest we ever got was our incorporation papers and an investor who wanted to fund the whole thing. Then, he used our business plan and did it on his own.

Even though nothing happened according to plan, the experience was extremely valuable. Attending this group fueled the greater purpose of pursuing a deeper relationship with Jesus. We were learning how to do it in the real world. So many great dreams and relationships were born out of this group!

Matrimony School

Remember that girl I mentioned earlier who was there on my first night with the college ministry? She was also a part of this business venture, and I was trying to get to know her.

We officially met on one of my first nights after returning to the group in April 2000. We had a guest speaker attend that night. She was a Messianic Jew, and she was performing a Seder (Passover) Meal. The Seder is the traditional Passover meal commanded in the Bible to commemorate the anniversary of Israel's miraculous exodus from Egyptian slavery more than 3,000 years ago.

We went through each meal stage as our teacher revealed the symbolism. We were sitting on the floor around the dinner table in Middle Eastern fashion, and I had the best seat in the house. I hardly remember anything about the meal, but what I do remember is the most gorgeous, big, blue-green eyes I had ever seen.

They belonged to a girl named Kelly. I tried everything within me to make sure she'd remember my name that evening by turning on the charm and trying to make her laugh.

After the evening was over, I drove my friend Jonathan home. As soon as we left, I told him, "I'm going to marry that girl!" At that moment, I knew God had heard and answered my prayer for someone to journey through life with me.

I'm thankful this night happened because I did not give the best first impression the first time Kelly saw me at the group when I visited in December. In my ignorance, I was clueless about what I did. I'll let her tell the story:

"I had been attending a college ministry group (led by people my age) for a few months and had made several new friendships. One night at our friend's house (where the college ministry was held), there were a few new people there that I didn't know.

There was one guy in particular who apparently grew up with many of the kids I had now become friends with. We were going around stating things we wanted prayer for, such as things we were struggling with in life, etc. This particular kid, David, began to say how he was having a hard time coming back home (he had been in Texas at an internship for a long time), and now all his friends had these new friends, which was weird. I now realize he maybe just felt like he no longer fit in, but at the time, I was thinking, 'Who is this idiot? I'm one of these new people he's talking about. I can't be friends with these people because they are 'your' friends? Rude.' He instantly turned me off. He would also carry this briefcase with a business plan everywhere he went. What 19-year-old did that? He was strange.

Then, sometime later, when he returned from his internship, the college ministry put on a Jewish Seder meal for us all to experience. A large table was set up in our friend's living room, and it was set up beautifully. I had brought one of my long-time friends, Juli, with me to this event, and lo and behold, guess who sits across from us...this David kid. I was like, ugh, but I wouldn't be rude.

Surprisingly, he started to make some jokes, and we laughed a little, but as dinner went on, he made my friend and me laugh out loud. I was like, 'This kid is hilarious,' and by the night's end, I saw a completely different side of him. I felt like we had become friends, and he was somebody I'd like to hang out with because he was so fun to be around and probably one of the funniest people I had ever met. The briefcase thing was still weird to me, though."

As we matured and grew, our time here began to wind down. Thankfully, Kelly didn't think I was so strange after all, and a new and wonderful season of our lives was just around the corner. On March 23rd, 2002, I married the love of my life, Kelly Dawn Mays. We had seven groomsmen and seven bridesmaids, many of whom were from this college-aged group. Many of them married each other as well. We all have amazing families and are still married to this day. This group, for all purposes, was matrimony school! Forget about all the e-match sites and dating apps out there. You'll meet the right person when you put yourself in the right place!

All the lessons and wisdom learned during this season would come into play many years later. My former roommates (now that we were all getting married and moving out) began attending my childhood church. This was my parent's church in the town of Derry. They invited me back to where I had tried to run from years earlier.

They had heard through the grapevine there was a new pastor in town. They said he was one of the funniest guys they had ever heard. "He could be a stand-up comedian," they told me. I had to go and listen to who this dynamic preacher was for myself. Little did I know that another fateful moment was just around the corner.

Chapter Seven: The Call

"There's your next youth pastor."

These are the words God spoke directly to my soon-to-be senior pastor, Shawn Lyons. It was my first time back to the church, and this is what Pastor Shawn heard as soon as he saw me come through the back doors. This made things incredibly awkward, considering they recently hired a new youth pastor. Also, signing up for vocational ministry as a pastor was not on my radar. In fact, when I was younger and attending Camp Mahaffey (the one where I broke my leg), someone spoke a prophetic word to me, stating that I would be in ministry and speaking to people. I didn't want anything to do with what this person shared.

I'll let Pastor Shawn share what he experienced that special Sunday:

His name was David

"It seemed to be a typical Sunday morning. The worship service had just started, and as I looked across the church sanctuary, I noticed that our youth pastor had just arrived at his regular seat. It was then that the normal Sunday service became anything but ordinary.

I felt a strong nudging in my spirit that someone had just walked into the building.

Sitting in the front row, I had to turn to see who walked in. I figured it must have been someone I knew as there was, all of a sudden, this great sense of excitement and expectation to see who it would be, but to my surprise, it wasn't anyone I knew. I didn't recognize this person or the young lady with him. It was then that I felt the Lord say, 'That's your next youth pastor.' I wasn't aware I was looking for our next youth pastor, but God knows everything there is to know about everything.

After the service, they introduced themselves, and shortly after, I began meeting with David and mentoring him. It wasn't long after that our current youth pastor decided to step down and take another position in another state. God had provided for us before we even knew we would need a new youth pastor, and his name was David Grimm. David served on staff with us for twelve years, and in those twelve years, we developed a wonderful relationship that we still share to this day, even though God moved him on to the next season of his life and ministry."

This was the last thing I wanted to hear, as I was deathly afraid of public speaking. I think, in some ways, ever since that moment, I was subconsciously running away from the church every chance I got for fear that I might actually have to do vocational ministry someday. I was not ready to hear this, and I'm thankful Pastor Shawn didn't share it with me immediately.

Kelly and I were newly married. We were renting our first little townhouse together and decided to make Harvest Church our home church. I was working at a juvenile delinquent rehabilitation program in the middle of nowhere in the wilderness of Pennsylvania. It was long-shift work. We lived seven days on and seven days off campus. Every two weeks, this was the rotation. Living with teenagers who had been adjudicated or abandoned by their families was a very challenging work environment. These kids did not desire to be here, and very few staff did either. The kids were tough, and the employees were almost unmanageable. Most of us were just like these kids when we were their age.

The day-to-day cadence was especially rigorous. We stayed in military-like bunkhouses and did outdoor PE and labor-intensive work projects throughout the year. We were regularly threatened, physically assaulted, or yelled at, all while living away from our families. As you can imagine, this wasn't the most fun work experience, especially during Kelly and I's first year of marriage. Although I know some couples who would enjoy being away from each other this much, I didn't want to see her for only half the year.

This job was challenging mentally, emotionally, physically, and spiritually. However, it paid the bills and provided the health insurance we needed.

About two years into this routine, I was growing desperately restless. This was a demanding pace to keep up with, and most staff lasted only a few months. Turnover was high. Time and time again, I job-hunted. Almost weekly, I would march down to the director's office with a two-week notice, only to feel a pause to wait and not go through with it. I was where I was supposed to be even when I didn't want to be there.

Daily, I spent time praying with these troubled teens. I discipled and encouraged them as I learned how to be in the trenches through everything they were going through. When my father turned me into the police, I thought I would end up in a place like this. Here I was, serving time alongside these kids just like I would have if I was arrested at seventeen. Working there was almost the same amount of time I would have been put away had I been adjudicated. God has a sense of humor!

Little did I know God was preparing me for something greater. I was in a training ground that would launch me and my wife into the subsequent critical season of our lives. I was going on three years at this facility and still needed to figure out what to do next. I was promoted from live-in staff to cabin director and could go home at night regularly.

I knew we were on the verge of a door opening and prayed daily that it would happen. It felt as if the door was padlocked, and we needed to kick it wide open. I prayed, "Lord, help us open this door, and please remove whatever barrier is keeping it shut. Help us do whatever you're calling us to do."

My heart was finally ready to hear and receive what was coming next. One day after church, Pastor Shawn approached me and said, "I'd like to go to lunch sometime this week with you if you're free one day."

That week, we met at a local restaurant in town, and the only thing I remember from our conversation was the simple statement he made to me. "David, be praying. I believe God has something for you here at Harvest."

It was a fresh wind to my longing heart. God had something for me! I prayed and prayed and asked year after year to clearly see what He had for me at the church. I was on the way home from work one day, and finally, out of frustration, I declared out loud in the middle of my car, "Lord, what am I supposed to do?!"

As clearly as I cried out loud, I heard an audible voice, a one-word response: "pastor." I almost wrecked my car as I whipped my head around to peer into the backseat. I thought for sure I had a stowaway in my car! In all seriousness, kids would often try to escape at my workplace. In fact, my fellow counselor and friend, Tom, had his car hijacked in the middle of the night by a kid who drove it to the next town. The boy traded the vehicle for a ride to Bronx, New York, where he was from. Remember, we were working with juvenile delinquents.

I turned my steering wheel, slammed my brakes, and skidded off to the side of the road. I literally just heard the word "pastor" out loud! God spoke to me, and I heard Him.

Later that year, the current youth pastor at Harvest Church resigned. I began serving part-time in youth ministry. That padlocked door was starting to open. I needed to learn how to preach and prepare lessons and sermons. This would come with time, practice, and mentoring.

Pastor Shawn always told me, "Don't share everything you know in one sermon. Keep them coming back for more." I didn't know much, so this was very difficult for me. The first sermon I ever preached was only 15 minutes long, and I didn't save much material for the next one. I'm pretty sure I shared everything I knew that first Sunday morning I preached. To this day, I only remember a little of what I taught. If this sermon was my first "pancake," it was a little overdone.

I knew two things for sure: the Word of God (the Bible) and how to hear God's voice. I served at the church part-time and still worked at this facility in the woods. This program where I worked was designed to purposefully put hardened and adjudicated youth through conflict to bring out their issues and force them to deal with problems as they break down their emotional barriers.

If the physical labor didn't wear you out, the time separated from your family did. If the separation from society didn't break you down, living with the complex personalities of each staff member would get to you fast! Many of these guys came from challenging backgrounds themselves. In fact, this job attracted many ex-military and retired special ops servicemen. If the personalities of your peers didn't frustrate you, the constant threat of physical attacks would keep you on edge. We had to learn how to defend ourselves without hurting the kids. It was called "Non-violent crisis protection intervention."

This was an exacting job. Every day I woke up, I wanted to quit.

I stuck it out in this program for three and a half years. I would never want to return because of the immense psychological pressure. However, this period was also the most rewarding and growing time of my life, and I wouldn't trade that for anything. I was forced to learn how to help the most down-and-out of our society who didn't want help, and in turn, I found myself being helped just as much as they were. I understood the importance of not disregarding challenging individuals or pushing them away. However, despite our numerous differences, I learned to collaborate with and extend love to them.

If you learn to persevere amid interpersonal conflict, the reward is great. You also learn that not only do you help the other person involved, but you are the one who gains the most significant transformation of growth spiritually and in character.

I only ran from difficult situations or problems when I was younger. It wasn't until I learned to stand right where I am and not run from struggle or conflict that I began to grow and build an overcoming mentality. I was experiencing the truth behind Paul's words in Galatians when he says, "And let us not grow weary while doing good, for in due season we shall reap if we do not lose heart." (Galatians 6:9, NKJV)

God finally had my attention, and I stopped running from the struggle for the first time. At the end of the three and a half years, the leadership at the facility came to me and shared that they would be eliminating my position. They wanted to promote me and offer a new job. This latest opening would require a lot more dedicated time. I couldn't work part-time at the church any longer in conjunction with this new opportunity they offered.

My next choice was easy. I wasn't sure how I'd get the health insurance we needed. I wasn't sure how I would make enough income, considering the church made it clear they could only afford me part-time. However, I knew God had called me to be a pastor. I took a step of faith and believed the Lord would provide for us. I learned if it's the Lord's will, it's the Lord's bill. Two weeks later, I was now in full-time ministry. If it's the Lord's vision, He'll bring the provision. I can't help it - I love these pithy and powerful sayings!

We moved into my parent's basement to get out of the rental, build some savings, pay off debt, and save toward our first home. When we made the career move, my pastor said, "I'm not sure how we're going to pay you." That didn't matter to me because the direction the Lord gave us was evident in my and Kelly's hearts. It was time for us to be in full-time ministry.

We didn't know how we would make enough money to live, but God did. It didn't matter if we knew because He knew. Two simple words became the defining reality over all the years in full-time ministry that were about to unfold. These two words superseded all other realities: "but God."

Lately, I have heard experts say NOT to use the word "but" when talking in the middle of sharing feedback or correction. Apparently, hearing that word negates or cancels out all previous words spoken before the word "but." For example, "You have a great personality, but you can also be overbearing sometimes." The compliment before the word "but" is now canceled. Once "but" is introduced, they will only remember that you think they are overbearing.

While I agree there may be better ways to use this simple word effectively, I claim it's still a powerful and effective word in certain concepts. I've seen it in action throughout the 12 years at Harvest Church. I've seen Pastor Shawn Lyons use it the entire time I've known him, and I've seen God do the miraculous by using this word correctly!

Think about Jesus' words in Matthew 19:26 (NKJV):

"But Jesus looked at them and said to them, 'With men this is impossible, but with God all things are possible.'"

But with God, ALL things are possible! This can mean many different things to many other people. Do any of these statements resonate with you?

- I would've lost hope, BUT God restored my hope!
- I would've lost my family, BUT God restored my family!
- I would've lost my life from this sickness, BUT God restored my health!

This was my baptism into full-time ministry. There wasn't enough money for me to come on full-time at the church, **but God** made it possible when it was not possible. Introducing **"but God"** into the equation negates anything before it. He can do anything! When Kelly and I stepped out in faith to do what we knew God was putting in our hearts to do, all of a sudden, more resources began to pour into the church.

The budget and balance sheets said there wasn't enough money, but we trusted God and acted. God's truth superseded the facts. He does stuff like this continually when we step out in faith to do what He's telling us to do. So many times, we give in to the facts in front of our faces because they cause fear, doubt, and disappointment. We can't imagine that there's any way out of our situation or circumstance because the facts say otherwise.

For example, it says in 1 Kings (a book in the Bible) that a widow woman was on her last measure of flour. There was a severe famine in the land, meaning it was everyone for themselves. The facts told her that she had enough for her and her son to make one last meal before they died of starvation. God's instruction was utterly contrary to the facts. God sent the prophet Elijah to this lone widow woman out of all the people in Israel that He could've chosen to send him. What was so unique and different about this woman from everyone else?

Let's look closely at this story from 1 Kings 17:10-14 (NKJV):

> *"So he arose and went to Zarephath. And when he came to the gate of the city, indeed a widow was there gathering sticks. And he called to her and said, 'Please bring me a little water in a cup that I may drink.' And as she was going to get it, he called to her and said, 'Please bring me a morsel of bread in your hand.' So she said, 'As the Lord your God lives, I do not have bread, only a handful of flour in a bin, and a little oil in a jar; and see, I am gathering a couple of sticks that I may go in and prepare it for myself and my son, that we may eat it, and die.' And Elijah said to her, 'Do not fear; go and do as you have said, but make me a small cake from it first, and bring it to me; and afterward make some for yourself and your son. For thus says the Lord God of Israel:*

'The bin of flour shall not be used up, nor shall the jar of oil run dry, until the day the Lord sends rain on the earth.'"

The little she had wouldn't have been enough anyway! It would've only been sufficient to prolong the inevitable one more day. Why are we so afraid to let go of the little we've been holding in our hands, even when it will never be enough? Thankfully, this woman in 1 Kings stepped out in faith at God's instruction. She was willing to hear and act on what God had to say.

Let's continue reading and see how God intervened due to her obedience:

"So she went away and did according to the word of Elijah; and she and he and her household ate for many days. The bin of flour was not used up, nor did the jar of oil run dry, according to the word of the Lord which He spoke by Elijah." (1 Kings 17:15-16, NKJV)

This woman's decision to act in faith by including God in the equation changed everything! Actions of faith and trust in our Heavenly Father move His heart to act on our behalf. The little she had ended up being MORE than enough. It became an abundance! There was enough for her, her son, and the prophet for most likely a few years! We know the famine lasted for three and a half years. (See James 5:17, NLT)

This is an incredible event. God's math is not our math. He can multiply anything with little to nothing if we trust Him with what we have. And, as we read in Hebrews 11:6 (NKJV), it all starts with faith: "But without faith it is impossible to please Him, for he who comes to God must believe that He is, and that He is a rewarder of those who diligently seek Him."

Without faith, you cannot please God. He wants us to put our trust in Him. He wants us to discover He is good and that He loves us. He wants to intervene on our behalf. We limit Him from intervening because we give Him no room. Faith opens the door for Him to step in. John writes in Revelation 3:20 (NKJV), "Behold, I stand at the door and knock. If anyone hears My voice and opens the door, I will come in to him and dine with him, and he with Me." Without faith, there is no open door.

God is knocking. Do we hear? Will we answer? We can say we have faith all day, but we can only prove it once we act in faith. Faith that has no action is no faith at all. Acting in faith opens the door for Him to come in.

James puts it this way: "Thus also faith by itself, if it does not have works, is dead. But someone will say, 'You have faith, and I have works.' Show me your faith without your works, and I will show you my faith by my works. You believe that there is one God. You do well. Even the demons believe—and tremble! But do you want to know, O foolish man, that faith without works is dead? Was not Abraham our father justified by works when he offered Isaac his son on the altar? Do you see that faith was working together with his works, and by works faith was made perfect?" (James 2:17-22, NKJV)

Faith is activated when it's put into action. We have been given examples throughout Scripture of those who have gone before us that pleased God, and they all had one thing in common: they acted in faith. So much, in fact, that God inspired the writer of Hebrews to list them as examples for us in the "Hall of Faith" chapter.

"Now faith is the substance of things hoped for, the evidence of things not seen. For by it, the elders obtained a good testimony. By faith, we understand that the worlds were framed by the word of God, so that the things which are seen were not made of things which are visible.

By faith Abel offered to God a more excellent sacrifice than Cain, through which he obtained witness that he was righteous, God testifying of his gifts; and through it he being dead still speaks. By faith Enoch was taken away so that he did not see death, 'and was not found, because God had taken him'; for before he was taken he had this testimony, that he pleased God. But without faith it is impossible to please Him, for he who comes to God must believe that He is, and that He is a rewarder of those who diligently seek Him.

By faith Noah, being divinely warned of things not yet seen, moved with godly fear, prepared an ark for the saving of his household, by which he condemned the world and became heir of the righteousness which is according to faith. By faith Abraham obeyed when he was called to go out to the place which he would receive as an inheritance. And he went out, not knowing where he was going. By faith he dwelt in the land of promise as in a foreign country, dwelling in tents with Isaac and Jacob, the heirs with him of the same promise; for he waited for the city which has foundations, whose builder and maker is God.

By faith Sarah herself also received strength to conceive seed, and she bore a child when she was past the age, because she judged Him faithful who had promised. Therefore from one man, and him as good as dead, were born as many as the stars of the sky in multitude— innumerable as the sand which is by the seashore." (Hebrews 11:1-12, NKJV)

Pretty impressive list, right? There's still more to come:

"By faith Abraham, when he was tested, offered up Isaac, and he who had received the promises offered up his only begotten son, of whom it was said, 'In Isaac your seed shall be called,' concluding that God was able to raise him up, even from the dead, from which he also received him in a figurative sense. By faith Isaac blessed Jacob and Esau concerning things to come. By faith Jacob, when he was dying, blessed each of the sons of Joseph, and worshiped, leaning on the top of his staff.

By faith Joseph, when he was dying, made mention of the departure of the children of Israel, and gave instructions concerning his bones. By faith Moses, when he was born, was hidden three months by his parents, because they saw he was a beautiful child; and they were not afraid of the king's command.

By faith Moses, when he became of age, refused to be called the son of Pharaoh's daughter, choosing rather to suffer affliction with the people of God than to enjoy the passing pleasures of sin, esteeming the reproach of Christ greater riches than the treasures in Egypt; for he looked to the reward. By faith he forsook Egypt, not fearing the wrath of the king; for he endured as seeing Him who is invisible. By faith, he kept the Passover and the sprinkling of blood, lest he who destroyed the firstborn should touch them. By faith they passed through the Red Sea as by dry land, whereas the Egyptians, attempting to do so, were drowned.

By faith, the walls of Jericho fell down after they were encircled for seven days. By faith the harlot Rahab did not perish with those who did not believe, when she had received the spies with peace.

And what more shall I say? For the time would fail me to tell of Gideon and Barak and Samson and Jephthah, also of David and Samuel and the prophets: ... quenched the violence of fire, escaped the edge of the sword, out of weakness were made strong, became valiant in battle, turned to flight the armies of the aliens. Women received their dead raised to life again. Others were tortured, not accepting deliverance, that they might obtain a better resurrection. Still others had trial of mockings and scourgings, yes, and of chains and imprisonment. They were stoned, they were sawn in two, were tempted, were slain with the sword. They wandered about in sheepskins and goatskins, being destitute, afflicted, tormented— of whom the world was not worthy. They wandered in deserts and mountains, in dens and caves of the earth. And all these, having obtained a good testimony through faith, did not receive the promise, God having provided something better for us, that they should not be made perfect apart from us." (Hebrews 11:17-32, 34-40, NKJV)

Wow! The world was not worthy of them because of how much faith they had in God. All of them were moved to act on the words and instructions He spoke to them. This is what moves the Lord's heart. This is no different for those who choose to follow Him today. These stories of men and women from long ago were written for us as examples of how we could live a life of faith.

This was the example set for me by my mentor, Pastor Shawn Lyons, over the entire 12 years I got to spend working with him side-by-side in ministry. It's challenging for me to summarize all that happened and all that I witnessed, experienced, and learned in one chapter. These stories would have to be a book on their own to do justice to all God accomplished in these years.

I will do my best to highlight the **"but God"** moments that profoundly impacted me and will echo in the halls of eternity, even though it won't be anywhere close to an exhaustive list.

The Witch

A coven of witches would've continued to perform their curses against the church, Pastor Shawn, and his family, **but God** restrained it after years of battling in prayer and holding his ground. It started on the first day after Pastor Shawn and his family arrived in town. The mother witch of the coven approached Pastor Shawn at a high school football game. She said, "I know who you are and why you are here. I'm going to run you out of town."

Thankfully, just the opposite happened. After years of battling in spiritual warfare, God intervened to protect our church and Pastor Shawn. Years later, we attended an annual outreach at a local mental institution. We would take gifts and sing Christmas carols to the patients every Christmas. Sometimes, we'd even get the opportunity to pray with them. They loved simply having someone who cared enough to come spend time with them.

We saw her in one of the wards. The same mother witch of the coven who had been performing curses against the church and had threatened Pastor Shawn was now a patient in the mental institution where we were ministering. Even though she wasn't receptive toward us, this encounter was a reminder of how God had protected and guarded Pastor Shawn, his family, and the church. I pray one day her eyes will be open and God will restore her mind. What a testimony that will be!

The Horrific Car Accident

Kelly and I received the dreaded call late at night. On the other end of the phone was our pastor. He said we better get to the hospital quickly. One of our youth group girls, Rachel, was just in a horrific head-on collision where she was thrown over 30 feet from her car. The doctors didn't think she would make it.

Jason (not his real name) was a student teacher who worked at our church's private school and happened to be driving on the same road where Rachel just had her accident only minutes before. He pulled over the hilltop to see a bruised couple in the other van. There was another car completely mangled and flipped on its side. No one was inside the vehicle. As Jason called 911, he searched and found Rachel unconscious, cradled in a ditch alongside the road.

Rachel's lungs and liver were lacerated. Bones were broken all over her body. The doctors had her sedated, and she was dying. They decided they would life-flight her in hopes that, by a miracle, they might save her through an experimental procedure using an ECMO machine. This machine was only meant to keep the body oxygenated long enough to harvest organs from donors. We were told by the doctors to get ready to say our goodbyes. We came to pray and to be there for her family, but her mom, Lynn, said with all confidence and no ounce of fear, "We dedicated her to the Lord as a baby, and we trust Him with her now." We all prayed for a miracle.

One of her brothers, Jon, and I went home to my parent's house, where Kelly and I lived, so he could sleep. Kelly, Rachel's parents, Pastor Shawn, and his wife Susan went to the Pittsburgh hospital to meet the life flight.

Shortly after we fell asleep, I was awakened by a nightmarish dream where Rachel was slipping into eternal darkness. Frankly, she was not living for God and probably didn't know Him. Her soul hung in the balance between Heaven and Hell.

I received a text from one of our youth leaders at about 1:00 a.m. who was going to the hospital with a group of our other youth leaders. Something told me they wouldn't make it there in time and needed to come to our house immediately so we could all pray. Once they arrived, I woke my dad, and we all battled in prayer together over the next hour.

Meanwhile, at the hospital, those who were already there experienced a cold drop in temperature in the halls outside the operating room. Death walked in. This may sound like a horror movie, but anyone who has ever experienced a tragedy like this one will tell you that this coldness can be physically felt. Just to verify, they checked the thermostat on the wall, and it was reading fine.

At the direction of Pastor Shawn, they all began praying as they walked up and down the hall. They declared the praises of God and asked Him for mercy. There was a popular Christian worship song at the time that became the theme song at the hospital that night. No one cared what anyone else thought. This was life or death, and they were going to Jesus, the One who conquered sin and death. He is the Resurrection and the Life, and they were imploring Him on Rachel's behalf.

At the same time that all this was happening, we received a report from Jason that he was also awakened by a nightmare. In the dream, he was in a dark room where the smell of burnt hair filled the air. "I desire to destroy young girls" was written on the wall in blood. That night, death was coming for seventeen-year-old Rachel, but God used His people to fight in the spiritual realm to save her life.

The Lord said, "Today is not the day, and Rachel will live!" To this day, the doctors do not understand how she survived. Not only did she recover, but she is married to a wonderful man named Josh with three beautiful girls of their own. They regularly attend the church and have successful careers. She should not be alive, **but God** brought her back from the grave!

Many individuals with physical severe bodily ailments received healing at the front of the church altar and in many hospital rooms. Rachel wasn't the only person who came back from death's door.

Many women were healed of infertility. One was a missionary's wife from Mexico. They had prayed and tried to get pregnant for years to no avail. That particular Sunday, they were visiting the church, and God led the pastor to call them forward, lay hands on her stomach, and declare her womb healed. A childless future was certain, **but God** said there would be children! They now have two beautiful grown daughters!

Another of these prayers for healing from infertility was for me and my wife.

Barrenness

We were married for seven years before God blessed us with children. For four of those years, we were actively trying to start our family. We tried everything and anything the doctors had to offer and tested us with. Nothing worked. We needed to see something more definitive. We had been praying and seeking God's will on what we should do.

One Sunday evening service, we had a guest missionary from India at our church. This man was prophetically gifted, heard clearly from the Lord on many occasions, and performed several big miracles. The missionary recounted crazy stories!

One winter, the house he and his family lived in had run out of oil in the tank that heated the home. They had no money to get it refilled. He prayed that God would supply their needs. The tank was never filled, but the heat worked the entire winter! He checked several times, and it was bone dry and empty.

The Lord told the missionary one day that it was time for him to return to India. In between stints, he would furlough here in the United States. This man heeded God's call and went to the airport with a suitcase in hand. The only problem is that he needed a ticket to get there. So, he sat and waited and waited some more. In his words, God would provide the ticket if he were to get back to India. A friendly businessman in a suit noticed that he had been sitting there awhile and approached him. The man began a cordial conversation. After talking briefly, he started asking about his plans. The missionary explained where he was going. The businessman then asked him, "What time is your flight?"

The missionary replied, "I'm not sure."

The businessman asked, "Well, what does it say on your ticket?"

"I don't have a ticket. I'm waiting for one." replied the missionary.

"Do you need a ticket to get there?" asked the businessman. "Yes," the missionary replied.

Immediately, the businessman got up, went to the counter, and bought our missionary friend a ticket. God provided just as the missionary believed He would.

When this man arrived in India, he wasn't sure where God wanted him to go. He prayed and asked the Lord. The missionary felt compelled to rent a bicycle and began riding it as far as he thought he was supposed to. When he reached a specific place, he stopped and just sat under a tree, waiting for the next set of instructions from the Lord. A man approached him and asked him who he was. The missionary shared, and the man asked if he could come immediately. There was a girl in a nearby village who was deathly sick. The missionary felt this was why he was here and went with the man.

When they arrived in the village, they were met by the girl's father. He explained they had done everything they could possibly do to help her. The medicine and the witch doctor couldn't do anything to save her. The missionary shared about the God he served who could heal the sick and bring the dead back to life. He then was given permission to pray for her in the name of his

God, Jesus. The girl's fever left her, and she was healed and rose off the bed. He discovered that the girl's father was the leader of their tribe in that village. He decreed that their village was now going to serve Jesus! The missionary obeyed all God's words and instructions, and the result was astounding.

This missionary told many other stories that were very similar to this one. Each one reflected an incredible, yet simple, act of faith that moved God's heart to do big things. Our faith was stirred, and we all desired to see God move, too.

At a moment in the service, he asked those needing prayer to come forward. Kelly and I, hand in hand, started to the front of the room to ask for prayer that we might get pregnant. At this point we had already been trying for 3 years. To be straightforward, this man had no clue why we were coming and what we were about to ask. No one shared this information with him. We took three steps forward. He looked straight at us and stated, "You are having twins, and the time is now." We stopped in our tracks, mouths gaping open, and turned immediately around to sit in our seats.

"What just happened?" We couldn't believe it. This man, a prophet and missionary, knew exactly what we wanted!

We moved into our newly built home next to my parent's house a few months later. A year after the prophetic word was given to us, we learned that we were pregnant with our first child, Tenley. This didn't come without cost. It took us a long time to get pregnant. So much so that we didn't know if it was going to ever happen. From when we got married to the time we got pregnant, seven years had transpired. My wife struggled with the idea that we might need to see a doctor to learn about our options since we weren't able to get pregnant. She thought that if we got help medically, then we weren't really trusting God to bring His prophetic word to pass in our lives.

Kelly sought out Pastor Shawn to get his counsel. He told her, "God is the only giver of life. Whether you use medicine or not, it's still up to the Lord." That was enough to help us understand that we needed help. All the tests came back normal for both my wife and myself. Kelly insisted the doctor give her treatment and soon thereafter, Tenley was in the oven!

What happened to twins? We didn't even care that the prophet got it "wrong." We were going to be having our first child in March of 2009! God had answered our prayer.

One year and a few months later, we were pregnant again. Things were not going so well towards the end of her first trimester of the pregnancy. My wife was having a lot of discomfort and pain. Then, she started heavily bleeding. We immediately thought she was having a miscarriage. As we headed to the hospital, we asked our family and our pastor to be praying.

The nurses initiated an examination of my wife, during which one of them mentioned the possibility of a tissue mass. To offer reassurance, they said that they frequently encounter such situations and that we would overcome them. However, these words did little to comfort us. As they left the room and we anxiously awaited the results, my phone rang. It was Pastor Shawn on the other end of the line. He said, "I know this sounds strange, but hold the cell phone to your wife's belly, and I'll begin to pray." The phone began to get hot! He then asked, "Did you feel that heat?"

I said, "Yes! It was intense."

"That's the healing" he replied.

Moments later, we would be transported to an ultrasound room where the results would be definitive. I watched the technician take readings repeatedly as if she didn't know what was happening. We were in this room for a long time! I watched as she was on one side of Kelly's stomach, taking pictures and measuring a little heartbeat. Then, I watched her move to the other side of the abdomen, taking more readings and measuring a heartbeat. Only this time, the heartbeat was a different reading. "What was happening here?" I asked myself.

The technician had a puzzled look on her face, and over and over, she kept taking measurements. She then quietly excused herself to go consult with the doctor. I had a feeling I knew what was happening, but I was hesitant to say it. Even though we were getting anxious waiting for the news, strangely, we had this underlying sense of peace at that moment. Whether it was a miscarriage or not, we would be ok. After what seemed like an hour, she finally entered the room again.

She smiled at us and said, "Well, you are not having a miscarriage. You are having twins!"

My wife looked sick. I started laughing, texting, and calling everyone I knew. As each person answered, I quickly exclaimed, "We're having twins!"

While we were still in that room absorbing the information together, God brought back the memory of what the missionary from India had said to us. "Twins, and the time is now!" It became clear at that moment that when he said "time," he meant "this season." This is the time (season) of having children, and in this season, we are having twins.

Asher and Hallie were born to us in March of 2011. It all came to fruition, and we laughed even more, stunned at God's revelation.

At that time, I was training for the Pittsburgh marathon. That night, when we got home, I ran five miles faster than I had ever run in my entire life because of the joy the Lord had put in my heart that day. It felt like my feet weren't even touching the ground.

Not even two years later, we had our fourth child, Sadie, in January 2013! Before, we had been childless and barren, **but God** decided we would have four children under four years. God can indeed bring dead things back to life.

Other Healings

We've seen plenty of other healings over the years. I remember an 80-year-old woman who wanted to take her own life due to overwhelming anxiety, fear, and mental anguish, triggered by relentlessly watching the news, who received healing and peace. Her mind was fully restored!

Another time, we saw a child with a hole in his heart healed before his surgery. We saw countless types of cancers disappear: prostate cancer, breast cancer, skin cancer, pancreatic cancer, brain cancer, and so on. Other heart issues, joints, aneurysms, strokes, eyesight, and allergies were healed. God was and is STILL a big God who can do anything when you let Him be a part of the equation by stepping out in faith to let Him work.

Never forget what a massive difference two words - **"But God"** - can make. I know I never will.

Chapter Eight:
Big God, Big Dreams

Why stop at physical healing? If we serve the God of the Universe who created everything we see, know, and don't see or know, isn't it reasonable to think He can do anything? He doesn't have a finite imagination and resources like us. He's infinite. Paul hints at God's all-encompassing power in the book of Ephesians when he writes, "Now to Him who is able to do exceedingly abundantly above all that we ask or think, according to the power that works in us." (Ephesians 3:20, NKJV)

Another incredible truth I learned while serving at Harvest Church all those years with Pastor Shawn is that God is limitless. So why do we limit Him? And how do we limit Him?

For starters, we limit God with thoughts such as, "This thing could never be possible." As the verse above says, God is able to do exceedingly and abundantly more than what we could dream up or imagine.

We may also limit God with our resources. We think things like, "I have to hold onto everything we have because we don't have enough to spare or give to the church or anyone in need." This limiting belief contrasts with Jesus' words in Luke 6:38 (NKJV): "Give, and it will be given to you: good measure, pressed down, shaken together, and running over will be put into your bosom. For with the same measure that you use, it will be measured back to you."

We even limit God with our most precious resource: our time. We subconsciously say, "There's not enough time in the day to pray, read my Bible, or go to church. We don't have time for those things in our lives. I have to get my kids to softball practice, soccer, gymnastics, and all their other extracurriculars. They have work, they have school, they have this party, and so much more." If all else fails, we may avoid church because we don't want to sacrifice our only day to sleep in. The excuses go on and on.

Since time is our most precious and fleeting resource, we can't afford to NOT give it to God by starting and ending each day in prayer and reading the Word. We can't afford NOT to give God at least one day out of the week by attending church with fellow believers. As the Word says, "And let us consider one another in order to stir up love and good works, not forsaking the assembling of ourselves together, as is the manner of some, but exhorting one another, and so much the more as you see the Day approaching." (Hebrews 10:24-25, NKJV)

Online church isn't the same. I'm thankful for the technology that makes online church possible for those who can't physically attend in person. Still, I don't believe anything can fully replace the experience of being together. You can't talk to each other and encourage each other on the screen projecting the service. You can't lay hands on one another in prayer over the screen, and the Bible is specific about this being a manner in which we receive healing. (See Mark 16:18 or James 5:14-15)

There are many other reasons why we are told to gather physically together. It's as if God knew one day we'd have an opportunity to no longer come together, so He had to tell us not to let this happen when we are tempted to be pulled apart. Imagine that! God knew something before we did?

We can't afford to NOT entrust Him with our time. Why? Because when we do, everything else falls into place. As we read in Proverbs, "In all your ways acknowledge Him, And He shall direct your paths." (Proverbs 3:6, NKJV) Another essential teaching comes right before this verse in Proverbs 3:5 (NKJV): "Trust in the Lord with all your heart, And lean not on your own understanding."

We can't possibly figure all this out. We are limited, finite beings. I don't care how talented, intelligent, funny, outgoing, or charismatic we may think we are. Our self-perception will never measure up to who God is and what He can do if we surrender our thoughts and imagination to Him. God is limitless, and He thinks infinitely. We are limited by the corners of our finite minds.

Now, don't get me wrong. We have incredible brains. Our minds and beings were made in the image of God. They were patterned after the way God works. Even still, ours are limited to the physical and what we know.

God's mind is the greatest super-intellect that has ever existed. He invented computing power and foresaw

ChatGPT before artificial intelligence was a human idea. There is no end to God's resources, and His power is limitless. So why would we not want to go to Him daily to seek wisdom, understanding, and direction for our lives? Keep in mind God invented what our lives would look like.

Psalm 139:1-16 (NKJV) paints a beautiful picture of the intimate manner in which God knew us before we knew ourselves:

> "O Lord, You have searched me and known me. You know my sitting down and my rising up; You understand my thought afar off. You comprehend my path and my lying down, And are acquainted with all my ways. For there is not a word on my tongue, But behold, O Lord, You know it altogether. You have hedged me behind and before, And laid Your hand upon me. Such knowledge is too wonderful for me; It is high, I cannot attain it. Where can I go from Your Spirit? Or where can I flee from Your presence? If I ascend into heaven, You are there; If I make my bed in hell, behold, You are there. If I take the wings of the morning, And dwell in the uttermost parts of the sea, Even there Your hand shall lead me, And Your right hand shall hold me. If I say, 'Surely the darkness shall fall on me,' Even the night shall be light about me; Indeed, the darkness shall not hide from You, But the night shines as the day; The darkness and the light are both alike to You. For You formed my inward parts; You covered me in my mother's womb. I will praise You, for I am fearfully and wonderfully made;

Marvelous are Your works, And that my soul knows very well. My frame was not hidden from You, When I was made in secret, And skillfully wrought in the lowest parts of the earth. Your eyes saw my substance, being yet unformed. And in Your book they all were written, The days fashioned for me, When as yet there were none of them."

God knows what's coming in our lives. He knew it before it happened and knows what is still yet to come. Why would we avoid going to Him daily? It's like consulting a manual for a microwave when trying to fix something wrong with your car. We're looking in the wrong places. We'll never find the answers looking elsewhere!

Big Dreams

The book of James begins with a reflection on the importance of wisdom. From there, James says to his readers, "If any of you lacks wisdom, let him ask of God, who gives to all liberally and without reproach, and it will be given to him." (James 1:5, NKJV)

The word "liberally" stands out to me here. What exactly does that word mean? In Greek, which is the original language that James wrote in, the word "liberally" is the word haplos (long sound over the letter "o"). The Greek looks like this: απλος. Haplos means "generously, without reserve, liberally." In other words, "liberally" and "freely" are synonymous.

So what does this mean for us? When we need understanding, when we need direction or advice on what to do in a particular matter or situation, when we're dreaming of big things, we need a big God to help us. And the fantastic thing is that God is there daily, waiting for us to come to Him at all hours and any moment to ask Him.

The author of Hebrews sums it up incredibly when he writes, "Seeing then that we have a great High Priest who has passed through the heavens, Jesus the Son of God, let us hold fast our confession. For we do not have a High Priest who cannot sympathize with our weaknesses, but was in all points tempted as we are, yet without sin. Let us therefore come boldly to the throne of grace, that we may obtain mercy and find grace to help in time of need." (Hebrews 4:14-16, NKJV)

When we come humbly to God, acknowledging our need for Him and His free gift of salvation through Jesus' sacrifice on the cross for our sins, we have no reason to fear approaching His throne to implore Him for mercy and grace to help in our time of need. God does not say you must appease Him first, that you're unworthy to approach Him, or that you must first bring a gift. Jesus did that for us on our behalf when we accepted His free gift.

We can now come boldly, knowing God has made a way for us. Not only this, but we can ask Him for wisdom any time we need it. When we do, He FREELY gives it. He does not look for a reason to say no. He does not say, "If I find fault, you get nothing."

In the New International Version (NIV), James 1:5 reads slightly differently: "If any of you lacks wisdom, you should ask God, who gives generously to all without finding fault, and it will be given to you."

Jesus removes our sin, guilt, and shame when we give it to Him. Now, the Father cannot find fault in us to withhold anything He longs to provide us. In this case, wisdom is freely ours when we ask, and He won't find a reason to keep it from us.

My senior pastor taught me that we serve the most creative Being that ever existed. We should, therefore, be the most creative people on this planet. For example, I don't know how to write a book. God gave me wisdom, and He's now helped me write four as of the writing of this book. Ask God, and He will provide the wisdom.

Around 2009, God placed a challenge on the heart of Pastor Shawn. He preached how we serve a big God who can give us big dreams, ideas, and abilities to do big things for His kingdom. Pastor Shawn then asked, why don't we ask Him for the creativity, ideas, and wisdom we need to accomplish these things? He knows everything there is to know about everything!

In the Old Testament, we see an example of God having a big plan to build the temple for His people, act as a central place of worship, and draw closer to Him. This task would be monumental and require tremendous skill, wisdom, and materials to build everything that would go into the temple. God provided the resources they needed for this big dream, as well as the knowledge and abilities of the individuals who would provide the skilled labor and understanding of how to build everything.

Don't take my word for it, though. Read the words of Exodus 36:1-2 (NIV): "'So Bezalel, Oholiab and every skilled person to whom the Lord has given skill and ability to know how to carry out all the work of constructing the sanctuary are to do the work just as the Lord has commanded.' Then Moses summoned Bezalel and Oholiab and every skilled person to whom the Lord had given ability and who was willing to come and do the work."

God put the ability in their hearts and minds to do the work! Wow. Can this still happen today? Yes, because God's word never changes or fails. It's eternal. As Jesus taught His disciples, "Heaven and earth will pass away, but My words will by no means pass away." (Matthew 24:35, NKJV)

Many in our church were inspired by this message. They began to heed the call to this word, asking God for wisdom, ideas, and creativity. One such couple who believed God could work powerfully began trusting Him to turn their business around. This couple went forward for prayer, and God spoke a word to them through Pastor Shawn. He said, "If you are faithful to trust God with what He tells you to give, He will bless your business." Soon thereafter, God put a call in their hearts. They obeyed, and shortly after, their business doubled! It didn't stop there. It happened many more times after that, and God continued to increase their business as they obeyed Him!

Another couple in the church had the idea to start a build-your-own Mexican food concept. God gave them the wisdom to build it along with the recipes and all the other things they needed to open this restaurant. The whole concept came together relatively quickly, and they opened their first "Madres Mexican" restaurant in Westmoreland Mall in Greensburg, PA.

Kelly and I got the "friends and family invite" for the soft opening. We were pregnant with our first child, and Kelly was preparing to "pop" as we quickly approached the baby's due date. We got in the long line and ordered delicious Mexican food just as we wanted. We both love spicy food, so we, of course, topped it off with the hottest sauce they invented at the time - the "Psycho" sauce.

We absolutely fell in love with this concept and the food. We also loved the family that started this unknown brand. As we were leaving the mall and raving about the experience, my wife's water broke on the way to the car. Baby Tenley was on the way! We joke that "Madres Mexican" was literally birthed in us.

By now, I had now been in vocational ministry for nine years. I had been faithfully serving as a youth pastor while learning side-by-side from my mentor about how to lead and love people. He challenged me daily to not limit God and to believe Him for the impossible. This sermon series, where he challenged us to ask God for dreams and creative ideas, was just the icing on the cake.

I took this word to heart, and I believed. It resonated deep inside me. In fact, I had been feeling that stirring inside me once again that something big was coming. I just had no idea what it was. I was feeling restless, and then this challenge from my pastor came. He ruined me because I could not stop thinking of big things and big ideas from then on. Still, to this day, I cannot stop dreaming. Why should I? We serve a limitless God who can do anything! Nothing is too difficult for Him!

Truthfully, I learned that if it's an idea too big for me to accomplish, it's a good indication that it's from God. When this happens, it's a reminder that we must trust in God and rely on Him for the provision, strength, and wisdom we need. God desires for us to trust in Him. It's an opportunity for us to conquer the fear holding us back.

We look for reasons and excuses not to move forward. We think, "What if it fails? What if I can't do it? What if I don't have enough money? What if (fill in the blank)?" Does this mean we foolishly charge forward without counting the cost? No! This means asking for WISDOM at every step of the journey—for planning, preparation, and provision. When we get an idea from God, we get to show Him that we trust Him and put our faith into action.

I began asking, "Lord, what should I do?" I would watch the families in the church who owned businesses. I remember thinking, "I want to be able to do what they do. I want to minister in the marketplace and reach people that others cannot reach other than through business."

I prayed and prayed and kept coming back to the idea of running a restaurant. For years, when I was younger, I would research various franchise models simply because I never ran a business independently. At least franchises could give you a model for how to do it. I researched multiple varieties of food franchises, including "Chick-fil-A."

It came down to two options for me. "Madres Mexican" or "Chick-fil-A." "Madres" was an idea simply because we loved the concept and the food and knew the family who started it. "Chick-fil-A" was another thought because we loved the food and how they did business. Plus, I knew our hometown's local owner, Todd, somewhat well. Many kids in our youth group worked at his restaurant. In fact, Todd's generosity the summer before is the main reason I latched onto the idea of pursuing this franchise.

We had created and hosted a sizable county-wide youth ministry outreach event at our church called "Summer Slam Fest." We prepared for 500 teens but had yet to learn how to get food for that many young people. Someone suggested I reach out to the local Chick-fil-A. They said they had heard of them supplying food for outreach and community events. I called the restaurant and asked if there was a time I could come meet Todd to present him with an idea. Todd was more than willing to meet with me.

I meticulously crafted my pitch and presentation and enlisted the support of my youth leader, Danny, to ensure everything was perfectly aligned. We sat and waited and felt nervous about this big request. Todd came out from the kitchen, greeted Danny and me, and asked how he could help us. I gave him the paper, shared our plan for the event, and said that we also needed help from him to supply sandwiches for 500 people. (Insert the hesitant emoji face here.)

There wasn't a pause or a "Let me think about this." Instead, Todd said one word: "Done." Then he got up from the table and said, "Just let my marketing director know, and we'll make sure we have them for you."

We were blown away and just laughed at the generosity we experienced. At that moment, I thought, "I need to be a part of this company somehow!"

Still, I hesitated to approach my pastor and let him know what I had been thinking and praying about. I didn't want him to think I wanted to quit working or serving at the church. I sheepishly shared my thoughts, and he said, "David, I had many opportunities presented to me in ministry to be in business and create income for my family. I just thought I had to turn them down to stay focused on what God gave me to do as a pastor. Looking back, I now realize He was giving me a way to provide for my family more effectively so I could remain serving Him in ministry."

They don't tell you in seminary that most pastors will probably never make six figures. They don't tell you that you might be unable to afford your student loans on a pastor's salary. They certainly don't tell you how many drop out of full-time vocational ministry in the first year because they can't afford to live and, therefore, need another job. Many pastors have second jobs to keep doing what God has called them to do.

He challenged me to go home and create a pro-con list between "Madres" and "Chick-fil-A" and then pray about it. That's exactly what Kelly and I did. The following week, it was apparent. I had one pro on the "Chick-fil-A" side and a host of others on the "Madres" list. I would have to learn from someone because I had never owned a restaurant. I have worked in various capacities in restaurants for years. I knew a lot about how things worked, but how would I run a Chick-fil-A without ownership experience? With Madres, I saw a family who started this concept and did it well.

We prayed that if this was supposed to be what God wanted us to pursue, He would make a way for us and make it clear. To be honest, God didn't make it entirely clear. I prayed and prayed some more that God would speak to me and tell me if this was what I should do. I wanted to avoid making a mistake and pursuing something that would keep me from being in ministry. After weeks, I heard no direction. I was praying some more, and finally, I felt the Lord nudge my heart. It was as if I heard Him say, "Do you want more?"

I had to ponder on that for a moment. I believe the Lord was challenging me. I could stay complacent doing what I am doing or go for more. This is a loaded word, and I'll get to unpack more later. I chose "more." Kelly agreed. I called the "Madres" restaurant family and pitched them my idea of being their first franchisee. On October 9, 2011, we were opening the first "Madres Mexican" franchise. After they thought and prayed about my pitch, they were on board.

I saw Madres Mexican as an incredible opportunity. I remember thinking about how I would love to be able to support ministers like my senior pastor, whose salaries can be a joke (no offense, Pastor Shawn). I know he's grateful, but it's not enough. The amount that these pastors and their spouses do and endure is unreal. No one can pay a pastor enough if they do what God has called them to do. The compensation is incomparable. Most will never make enough to support their families effectively because they pastor in smaller rural communities. Most churches are not mega-churches where there are plenty of resources.

According to a recent article by Barna (an independent research group), only two in five "practicing" Christians offer at least 10% of their annual income as a "tithe." Here's an excerpt from that article [4]:

> "When it comes to generosity within the local church, just 21 percent of Christians set their church giving at 10 percent or more of their income. Typically, their giving varies (37%), while one-quarter (25%) doesn't give to their church at all. Practicing Christians are much more likely to set their giving to at least the customary 10 percent tithe (42%), though that means the majority of practicing Christians is still giving in lower or less predictable amounts."

Tithes and offerings are a Biblical principle. We're called to give our resources to the work of the Lord through the church. This includes using these resources to fund the church's pastorate to equip the saints. Yes, I believe God will supply all their needs according to His promise in Philippians 4:19. However, I still wanted to be a part of supporting the men of God who sacrifice so much to bring the truth to people that changes lives for eternity. Sacrifice is an understatement!

On that promising October day, the Grimm family opened the first "Madres Mexican" franchise in the Monroeville Mall food court. Monroeville is a suburb outside of Pittsburgh. The training at their restaurant lasted about nine months, and I was grateful. It took us that long to discover how we would pay for this venture.

---

[4] https://www.barna.com/research/what-is-a-tithe/

Restaurant equipment is expensive! We were in business after we took out a home equity line of credit and added some extra insurance money we collected from a house damage payout!

We negotiated the lease, rented the space, became a self-contractor on the job, organized the free labor (not counting the promise of free "Madres Mexican" for life), did the build-out, set up the equipment, hired and trained our "Burrito Builders." That was all just within the first month! That was hard work, but nothing compared to what we were about to experience.

Meanwhile, I was still serving at the church. I was now one day a week in the office and still preaching on Wednesday nights with the youth group. That week before the grand opening, Pastor Shawn came into my office and said, "It's a good thing you are opening this restaurant." I looked puzzled because I thought, "I'm grateful too." However, I had a feeling we were thinking different things.

Pastor Shawn proceeded to share that there wasn't enough money for the church to keep me on staff. That was a gut punch to the stomach, to say the least. I sat there stunned for a bit. I was hoping we'd continue to have my ministry income (even if it was part-time again) so that it would be a supplement to what we'd generate at the restaurant.

I shouldn't have been stunned because I knew exactly why. Our church had just been through the most extensive shaking we had ever experienced in our 30-plus years of existence. An individual in the church was going through a challenging time in his personal life. This man had served at the church in many different capacities and was one of Pastor Shawn's trusted friends. These men had experienced so much in ministry together all over the world. A series of hardships started in his life with his health and job, and he began acting differently toward all of us. We couldn't put our finger on exactly what was going on with him internally. A sense of jealousy and bitterness started brewing inside him. Despite his prayers, good things were happening for others and not for him. At least, this is what he focused on, even though God had done incredible things for him as well. He was frustrated. In fact, the church was in the healthiest place it had ever been, and we were making a tremendous positive impact in our community and around the world with our outreach ministries.

He did not appropriately deal with these thoughts and feelings. He started a faction behind the scenes with other families that attended the church. He spread lies about all of us on staff and held secret meetings with these families to share these lies. It all finally came to a head shortly after all this started. A confrontation took place where we addressed these lies and wrong behaviors. As a result, those families, including his own, decided to leave the church.

They continued spreading rumors about us everywhere they went and caused so much unnecessary damage. They didn't come to each of us first to discover if what they were hearing was the truth. Instead, they foolishly chose to believe everything they were told at face value. They could have spared many from heartache and emotional and spiritual damage, including their own. Unfortunately, they caused great harm, and it's hard to describe how far it reached for many years beyond.

Some, like their own families, never recovered. Many got divorced and experienced strange, undiagnosed diseases and illnesses. This man convinced himself he was doing the right thing at the time, and later, we discovered he battled turmoil within himself for years afterward.

Many years later, Pastor Shawn got a phone call. On the other end of the phone was this man's wife. She bashfully shared that her husband requested to see Pastor Shawn at the hospital. He was on his deathbed. He had contracted MRSA in his spine. They had to open him up, shave all the fins off his vertebrae, and clean him out. He was recovering from the operation, but the end prognosis wasn't looking good.

Thankfully, Pastor Shawn did the hard work of forgiving these people for all the unnecessary harm they caused him, his family, and many in the church, including mine and Kelly's family. He brought himself to visit this once-trusted friend who had now become a betrayer. In that hospital room, the man poured out his heart, confessed his sins, and asked for forgiveness for what he had done. Pastor Shawn could say that he had forgiven him and had the opportunity to pray with and for him. A few days later, when he passed, I believe He went home to be with Jesus because he made his heart right. I told you the work and sacrifice pastors do cannot be compensated.

However, this reconciliation didn't happen for some time, and because of what these people had done, there was no more money to keep me on staff. Thank the Lord we decided to open this restaurant at the time we did! At least, we thought at the moment that the timing was fortunate.

Chapter Nine:
Season of Testing

There have been moments when I believed I wholeheartedly trusted God. Then, something would come along that I never faced or experienced before, and that trust was put to the test. Not just put to the test but run through the mud, stomped on, and beat mercilessly to the point of barely being able to feel a pulse. In these seasons, I discovered just how much I really trusted in God.

I would ultimately learn that God is faithful in every circumstance. This truth has been a key learning in my years of ministry. In those times when you can't see God's hand or are searching for God's answers or provision, and it seems like it isn't there, trust still matters. God is always faithful, and His promises never fail. Paul reminds us of this in Philippians 4:19 (NKJV) when he writes, "And my God shall supply all your need according to His riches in glory by Christ Jesus."

Things were going very well shortly before we launched our restaurant and the attempted coup at the church. We had our first three children: Tenley, Asher, and Hallie. We had a beautiful home beside my parent's house next to a nature reserve built by Arnold Palmer. (This land was my grandparent's former farm).

Our church and youth group were growing. We planned to start a new business, and life was good. Then, one day, a lady from our church entered my office. She was an elderly woman who asked if she could share something she believed God gave her. It was a verse in the Psalms. It feels very loaded when people come to you and ask things like this. For example, if you say, "No, you can't share it," what will they do? I was hesitant to hear, and I had already determined I would contemplate and pray to determine if what she was telling me was really from God. She read the following verse: "Show me a sign for good, That those who hate me may see it and be ashamed, Because You, Lord, have helped me and comforted me." (Psalms 86:17, NKJV)

She shared that God wanted me to have this verse to pray and hold onto through what was happening or about to happen. It felt very ominous, and I did not like it one bit. She proceeded to ask, "Is everything okay with you? Is there anything difficult going on?" I had to think about that for a moment.

I contemplated how, three years prior, my Mom, Barbara, had battled breast cancer. She endured numerous treatments and rounds of radiation, and our family fervently prayed for her recovery. Despite our hopes and prayers, my mom still had to undergo these challenging treatments. After a couple of years, we received the news that she was in remission, and my parents, Dennis and Barbara, were finally regaining a sense of normalcy. We just had our first child, Tenley, and were in celebration mode as a family.

However, the celebration was short-lived. That summer, my dad became ill with a disease that severely impaired his breathing ability. We suspected it might be a cold or a respiratory infection. It quickly became apparent that his situation was much more severe. My father struggled to catch his breath, rendering him unable to speak. He could hardly move for lack of energy and getting winded.

My mother insisted that he go to the emergency room. When the medical team conducted tests and received his blood work results, the doctor immediately recognized that something was seriously wrong. They arranged for his transfer to Shadyside Hospital in Pittsburgh, a facility renowned for its expertise in cancer treatments. There, the medical team deemed performing a bone marrow biopsy imperative. Two days later, he was diagnosed with Acute Myeloid Leukemia, which had taken over 70% of his blood production. The doctor told us he had a 30% chance of surviving the treatment. Not the disease itself but the supposed cure.

This was brutal and devastating news. I vividly recall when my mom, dad, and I sat down with the doctor, attentively listening as he outlined the potential risks and challenges associated with the treatment plan. I thought for a brief moment: "Lord, just please take my dad. Don't let him go through this suffering." As I silently prayed, the overwhelming peace of God flooded my mind and heart. God told me, "It's going to be okay." My dad heard the same thing. Otherwise, letting the disease take its course would have been better.

There was a man on his hospital floor with the same diagnosis. He was a bodybuilder and only half my dad's age. He only lived a few weeks after he contracted the disease, which shows you how lethal it really is. While all forms of leukemia are dreadful, this type ranks among the most aggressive.

Of my dad's six living siblings, his sister was the best match for his blood and donated her stem cells. They killed off his bone marrow, and the stem cells regenerated in his dead marrow to produce healthy blood again. The treatment itself was a miracle!

I'll skip the details, but after four months of trips to the hospital to visit and pray with my dad weekly, the doctor told him something you don't typically hear doctors say. The doctor was a Christian, and he and my dad often talked about the Lord. Much to our surprise, the doctor told him he was cured! Fourteen and a half years later, from the time of this writing, they are still monitoring his blood work, but the cancer has not returned.

I am in awe. My dad went from having a 30% chance of surviving the treatment to being 100% cured. Caring for my parents was a challenging season, but God brought us through.

When the woman entered my office to share this verse from the Book of Psalms and asked if anything difficult was happening in my life, these were the first thoughts that flooded my mind. Although they had transpired a few years prior, they were indeed difficult at the time. Moreover, the trials still felt fresh. I had three kids in diapers, and I felt like a zombie because I hadn't slept since they were born. "Yes, it's hard right now!"

This was simply "life," though, wasn't it? Life throws curveballs, and we understand that having babies changes everything. We had already weathered our fair share of challenges. How much more difficult could it become?

If only I had known what was lying ahead. Looking back at what I know now, this woman spoke prophetically about what would soon transpire.

Madres Mexican at Monroeville Mall

We were getting ready to launch our restaurant in Monroeville Mall. I spent September 2011 gearing up for the grand opening. I became my own contractor. My dad, some long-time friends, and I built out the lease space and transformed this near-empty shell into a build-your-own Mexican restaurant. This woman walked into my church office just a few months before. I had forgotten all about what she said. I discounted it because nothing happened.

Just one week before the grand opening on October 9, 2011, it dawned on us that making this restaurant financially viable was not a luxury - it was a necessity. We were banking on this venture to become our primary source of income. The first three months were golden! I started making plans to open three more "Madres." We'd be set for life based on these sales.

Then January hit.

Suppose you know anything about retail sales in a mall. In that case, you know the first week of January is typically profitable for mall sales. Then, kids return to school, and 90% of your clientele stops spending money. They may have post-Christmas returns to make, but that's about it. Except for the mall employees taking advantage of their generous discounts, it was crickets, and their orders were barely enough to keep the business alive.

Things turned worse when we received some disconcerting news in January. Chick-fil-A was pulling out of the food court. When I first heard the news, a nervous 'gulp' seemed to lodge itself in my throat. Chick-fil-A only exits a location if sales and foot traffic have sharply declined. It was an ominous sign. Nevertheless, we were bound by our lease and determined to persevere and make our business thrive.

Sales were slow at the beginning of 2012. I thought to myself, "No problem! February is right around the corner." The arrival of a new month did nothing to help our plummeting bottom line. February is historically the worst sales month of the year for malls. As March rolled around, we anticipated a steady uptick in business. True to our hopes, sales began to rebound, and it felt like we were back in the race.

I worked from open to close Monday through Saturday, with the exception of Wednesday evenings, and my wife ran the store on Sundays so I could go to church and spend the day with our children. I volunteered at the church, serving the youth one day a week, even though I didn't get paid. I juggled multiple responsibilities, from preparing food in Madres' kitchen and serving hungry patrons to crafting my Wednesday night sermons during breaks. It was undeniably exhausting, but our teamwork made it all possible. We were fortunate to have exceptional "Burrito Builders" (as we affectionately called our employees) who we could always count on.

Then, during the spring of 2012, the unexpected happened. The following article from the WTAE Channel 4 News website explains it all. [5]

> *"The gunfire erupted at a Pittsburgh-area shopping center on Saturday at 7:33 p.m., sending shoppers running for safety.*
>
> *The mall and Forbes Hospital's emergency room were placed on lock down as police searched for the gunman. Police went to the store to evacuate the mall.*
>
> *Jesse Miller, a spokesman for Forbes Hospital, says detectives told the hospital to lock down its emergency room until they were certain the shooter had been captured.*
>
> *Officers and agents from 15 different agencies were called in to conduct the search for the suspect and assist with the incident. They went store by store and floor by floor.*
>
> *Pittsburgh's Action News 4's Courtney Fischer spoke with an eyewitness of the shooting who says he saw a man take out a black gun and point it 'at a group of people.'*
>
> *Shoppers described chaos as shots rang out.*
>
> *'I grabbed my friend and said, 'Let's go,' and said, 'We're out of here,' Mitchell Swann, 18, of Rankin, told the Pittsburgh-Tribune Review. He said he heard several shots.*

---

[5] https://www.wtae.com/article/monroeville-mall-suspect-has-juvenile-past/7470040

Yvette Jackson, 38, of North Braddock, was attending a birthday party at Giggles and Smiles, a fitness and fun center for children.

'We saw a lot of running, a lot of chaos,' she told the newspaper. She said she and other patrons were locked in the store for about 45 minutes until police came and let them out.

Pennsylvania native and ex-NFL quarterback Terrelle Pryor tweeted he was at the Monroeville Mall and saw two people get shot. 'Damn was just in Monroeville Mall and just saw 2 ppl get shot,' he tweeted. 'They are letting guns go in there.'"

After this incident, the mall became a ghost town. There wasn't any amount of marketing or hustle that was going to solve this problem. Trust me, we tried it. Customers did not want to shop somewhere they felt unsafe. There were plenty of other options.

Before we knew it, we were three months behind in rent. We stopped paying ourselves and worked as many hours as possible. Thankfully, my wife still had her full-time job working as an abstractor. At the time, her income was enough to at least pay for our basic four-wall needs at home. I wasn't making money but could pay the restaurant bills (minus the rent). I could also eat delicious Madres Mexican food for lunch and dinner daily.

In other words, we were still doing okay. That is, until one evening when my wife came home after her 45-minute Sunday commute from the restaurant.

All three of our kids were tucked away in bed. I expected Kelly to come through the door, and we'd sit down to watch a TV show together before we crashed and woke up at the crack of dawn only to repeat the cycle. She made a beeline upstairs without uttering a word.

As I sat on the couch to relax, something was flung out of haste from behind me onto my lap. It was a plastic stick with two little lines, and my wife panicked. On the way home from work that day, she realized she had been "late." I don't mean she was late to return from work. I'm talking about a three-month delay of a different kind!

It's easy to judge, but our lives were moving at breakneck speed, and we barely had time to pay attention to such matters. I shot straight up and felt sick. Immediately, I hunched over and declared, "I need to talk to Pastor Shawn."

We were elated but filled with panic, sadness, and worry in the midst of our joy. To put it bluntly, we were a mess. How could this happen? Well, we all know how, but still, this wasn't planned! We were hanging on for dear life financially, given all that was happening in our business, in addition to the fact that we had three children in diapers. How could we do this? We wanted to celebrate our family's fourth and newest addition. Still, we also felt somber due to our lack of time and financial resources. We alternated between laughing and crying.

We didn't know it then, but God knew we needed this fourth baby girl! We fondly refer to Sadie as our comic relief. We tried, prayed, and fought to have the other three, but she was the best surprise ever. We prepared and adapted to welcome our fourth member into the mix. We now had four kids under four years old!

The fall season of shopping rolled around. People were still skeptical, even with the new police substation at the mall. Traffic slowly started returning, but we needed much more to get us out of our three-plus months' worth of lease back payments. We barely met obligations and still weren't making enough to pay ourselves. We were feeling the stress of being at a loss. We prayed and asked God for wisdom and a miracle.

My mom's breast cancer had returned during this time, but not how you'd expect. One day, as I was at the restaurant, I got a call. "Mom is being taken to Shadyside Hospital in an ambulance."

"What? I know she has been having back pain, but what's going on?" I asked.

They were taking her to undergo a series of tests. A massive tumor was discovered that had eaten away a part of her spine. It was breast cancer causing all the pain. It was back and metastasized to this part of her body. They planned emergency surgery. I escaped from the business and went to the hospital just in time to pray with my mom. We asked God for a miracle.

The doctors removed the tumor and installed a plate to hold her spine firm. In the follow-up, they did more tests and discovered the cancer had spread to other various parts of her body and brain.

She had come home after recovery. My mom and dad loved to walk next door to visit and spend time with the kids. This time, the visit was not so joyful. Thankfully, the surprise news of our fourth child was able to cheer them up, even if to take their minds off the situation for a moment.

Throughout the remaining months of her treatment, I believed with all my heart that God would heal my mom. Whether it be through medicine like my dad or an absolute miracle, I knew it would happen. I believed. Why shouldn't I? I had seen cancer after cancer miraculously disappear in so many lives! God could do anything, and I knew it.

It was early October 2012, and my mom was back in the hospital. I asked my pastor if he'd go with me to pray, battle this cancer once and for all, and declare a miracle over my mom. She asked in her frail voice, "Do you think I will get healed?" In all certainty, I told her, "Yes, Mom, I know God is going to do it."

As we left the hospital, I had a reserved thought and asked, "Pastor Shawn, do you think my mom is going to get healed?" I just now realized he never answered when we were inside the building. He could barely look at me. No words came out, and tears filled his eyes. He didn't need to answer. I knew what he was telling me, and he was right. I didn't want to admit what was in my heart.

I was outside on a Sunday playing with the kids only a few weeks before this moment when she could still walk. I saw my mom skinny and weak with her head covered, and I remembered God told me, "I'm taking her home." I quickly dismissed this as thoughts of doubt as I did not want to admit defeat.

"She is going to make it. She is going to watch my kids grow up. She is an artist, and I always had plans for her to teach my kids how to paint one day. My mom will not leave this earth and not see her grandkids grow up." I pondered these thoughts many times before.

She was released to hospice care at the house shortly after turning for the worse. At my parents' home next door, we celebrated my mom and dad's 33rd wedding anniversary on October 7, 2012. We didn't have anything to give, but we could share our newly picked out baby's name for our soon-to-be newborn. We decided to call her "Sadie Ann," after my mom's middle name. It brought a smile to her face when she first heard the news.

Many people came and went the following two days. She asked, "Do you still think I'm going to be healed?"

"Yes, Mom," I would reply, not having the heart to say otherwise.

Two nights later, we were all together as my mom was now heavily sedated. I left for the night to go home and get a shower. My dad leaned over to her and whispered, "Honey, just like you've trusted God with everything else in your life, it's time to trust God with your breathing." She breathed a couple more breaths and then none.

I got the call at home. Though filled with tears of joy and sadness, my instant response was, "Mom made it home!"

I couldn't help but think, "Mom is now in Heaven saying to herself, 'Why did I not let go sooner?'" I believe my mom did get healed that day. She was made perfect in

Heaven. No more suffering, sadness, or tears. She made it home to be with Jesus.

I was still angry, mad, and confused, but also glad she wasn't suffering any longer. The following weekend was a whirlwind for her memorial, where we got to host one last art gala full of her artwork. She would've loved for everyone to appreciate her art. We couldn't think of a better way to celebrate her life.

The following Monday, I was back opening the doors to the business, unable to grieve in front of happily paying guests. This was hard. I was angry at God for not healing her here, yet I was also relieved for my mom at the same time. It's okay to share what we feel and think with God. He knows it already, after all. God is big, and He can handle it. He wants us to bring it all to Him. I Peter 5:7 (NKJV) says, *"casting all your care upon Him, for He cares for you."*

As badly as I wanted my mom to be healed on this planet, she wasn't. After her homecoming, I wrestled with doubt in my prayers and struggled for a long while. Looking back, I believe God was preparing me to see how big He is and how much He truly cares for us. I learned that His plan for my mom did not reflect His plan for me. The Bible tells us in Ecclesiastes 3:1-2 (NKJV), *"To everything, there is a season, A time for every purpose under heaven: A time to be born, And a time to die; A time to plant, And a time to pluck what is planted;"*

We like to talk about the time of being born and having babies. We don't like talking about the other guarantee. We all have an expiration date. When it comes, will we be ready?

Miracles

I have learned a funny truth about miracles. They don't always happen. When they do, it's when you need them. Think about what constitutes a miracle. For a miracle to happen, you must face a desperate situation or need. When an answer comes supernaturally in an otherwise impossible manner, it's called a miracle.

Webster defines a miracle like this: "an extraordinary event manifesting divine intervention in human affairs."

In a desperate situation, something greater beyond earthly capabilities is needed to bring the answers. This was where Kelly and I found ourselves over the next three years. The following is a highlight reel, but not an exhaustive list, of all God did in our lives during this season. Sharing the following stories is extremely humbling. It requires us to admit how desperate we were and incapable of solving the problems we faced.

We couldn't possibly do any of this on our own! God is good.

We received a certified letter in the mail shortly after my mom's homecoming. It came from the mall property management company and stated that we would have our doors padlocked by December 24, 2012, if we didn't pay up all our back payments on the lease.

Were we living in Charles Dickens's "Christmas Carol?!" They had to pick Christmas Eve? Were these people for real?! Who are they, Ebenezer Scrooge?! This was our new reality, and we could do nothing about it.

By November 2012, Christmas season shopping had begun, and the certified letter was looming over our heads. We had no idea what to do because we couldn't make these shoppers manifest, but strangely enough, they did. In fact, this December was one of the busiest holiday shopping seasons the mall had ever seen. In just a few short weeks, we were able to pay back over $20,000 just in time to remain open past Christmas. It was a true Christmas miracle.

Sales were growing again, and we were figuring out a new routine without my mom just two months after she went home. It was the day after Christmas, and we had reason to celebrate again. And we did! Our family has a yearly tradition of going to a movie the day after Christmas. It's something we all look forward to. Our family members who travel to Pennsylvania reunite over the holiday and make the movie night out a priority. We always have at least twenty people attend.

We exited the theater and went into the mall as soon as the movie ended. This was the same mall where our "Madres" restaurant was located. We were shocked to find a ghost town with caution tape and police blocking every entrance. What happened?!

Our mall made national news AGAIN! A flash mob of 100 teenagers organized a plan to terrorize the mall that night. They ransacked the retail stores, went on a theft spree, overturned kiosks, attacked patrons, and destroyed property. People were afraid, and traffic dwindled once more. Our employees locked themselves in the back-office area of the restaurant that night and couldn't get a hold of us due to the lack of cell service in the theater.

A few months later, another shooting occurred in the mall parking lot. Sales plummeted even more, and so did our income. We were back to paying our employees but not paying ourselves. I worked 80 hours a week without income and was trying to recoup.

Of course, the grinder pump that rids our house of sewage and wastewater also broke around the same time.

We needed help to get the money to fix it. We could barely afford groceries and could no longer take showers or use the water. All six of us had to brush our teeth outside with a hose in the middle of the snow in winter. Seeing four little ones bundled up and brushing their teeth was quite the sight. It was the straw that broke me. I was lost. I couldn't understand.

Where we lived, it was rural, and burning your trash was acceptable. I took a couple of bags from our kitchen to our shared burn pit with my dad. Standing in the snow watching the fire, I looked at the night sky. The snow was bright all around, and I desperately prayed, "Lord, show me a sign of favor for good." Just then, I saw a shooting star streak across the sky, filling me with hope—even if only for a brief moment.

Again, these are just the highlights and only some of the details of our struggles during this time. Why am I listing all these horrible things? To make you feel pity? No. I have to tell you about the struggle and the crisis we found ourselves in so you can understand the victory in the turnaround.

What happened next was nothing short of miraculous.

Loaded Down Suburban:

Between Kelly's income, my lack of income, and our recurring business expenses, we could barely pay our personal bills. We had our fourth baby, and there were days we had to decide to buy groceries or pay the bills. One day, it all came to a head, and my wife and I didn't know our next move. We went to church on a Wednesday night and asked for prayer. We were humiliated. We were both broken. We went forward and asked God for help.

That Saturday morning, a friend of ours showed up in our driveway in her Suburban. She told us she had woken up the night before, and God told her to write a comprehensive grocery list. Her Suburban was loaded down! Her grocery list was detailed. The brand of shaving gel I used, the unique formula my youngest daughter was on due to her milk allergy, and a case of Keurig cups. That last one was strange because we didn't own a Keurig, but much to our surprise, my dad came over that same day with a new Keurig for us. (It was an early Christmas gift).

The list goes on. In addition to everything else, our friend from church also purchased us new Egyptian cotton sheets for our queen-sized bed. It's important to point out that this woman knew nothing about our specific needs. How did she know exactly what products to buy, down to the precise brand? How was she aware that my dad would give us a Keurig? That day, she gave us enough food to sustain us for over three months! Our kids were jumping and running around the piles in the kitchen of all their favorite snacks. It was quite the site to behold!

I was incredibly thankful for her generosity, my wife admits that this act of kindness healed something broken inside of her heart she didn't realize needed healing.

Food Credits:

Things were still slow at the business though. However, I got a call from our food supplier at Gordon Food Service one day. Somehow, a credit due to overpayment gave us almost a month's worth of free food for the restaurant. Amazingly, this wasn't the only time I would get this call. It happened several more times over the next few months.

Christmas time:

We had no idea how we would buy our kids Christmas gifts this season. There was no earthly way we could afford to get them presents. My wife, Kelly, tells the story so well since she lived it firsthand.

"Every day at work, I would have to walk through an overpass from one part of the courthouse to get to the tax office in another building of the courthouse. At Christmas time, they would have a huge table set up with children you could sponsor and purchase gifts for. I believe it was through 'Angel Tree.' These children's parent(s) were imprisoned or possibly didn't have parents and were just part of the system.

We were really struggling financially and didn't know how we would buy our four kids presents that year. The first day I saw the table set up to sponsor kids, I saw a family of three siblings and felt a nudge in my heart to take their names and buy them Christmas presents. I quickly squashed that feeling, thinking, 'That's crazy because I don't have money for my own kids this Christmas.'

The next day, I had the same feeling when I passed the table. I got annoyed and was like, 'God, I can't support these kids, you know that.' However, even saying that under my breath didn't bring me peace, and I thought, 'If their names are still here by Friday, I'll take them.' I saw the names the next two days, getting more stressed about it, and knew when I walked over Friday afternoon, there they would be.

Friday came, and I took their names with the suggestions of gifts attached to them. I had $150, which would've been all the money I had to split between our four kids for Christmas, and having that money to spend for Christmas meant I was choosing to be late on a couple of our bills in the first place. I split the $150 between the three siblings and felt such peace, being a blessing to another family that was obviously less fortunate than we were. I felt like I was listening to the Lord asking me to give. I had reasoned in my head that my kids were still very young and wouldn't really recognize not having a Christmas.

That Sunday, we came to church, and a couple my parent's age approached us. They said they felt like the Lord told them they needed to buy our kids their Christmas presents this year. They asked me to give them four to five suggestions for presents for each of our children. I was shocked and humbled. I believe the Lord tested us to see if we would be faithful with the small things in the hard times. My kids had such an amazing Christmas with so many presents! They never *knew until years later that they weren't from us when we told them the story of how God provided for us when we were obedient to trust Him."*

Unexpected product:

On another day, a new restaurant outside the mall moved into our food court. They took a look around and came over to us. They told us they were switching from Coke products to Pepsi products, noticed we were the only ones who sold Coke, and asked if we wanted all their unused products. Thanks to this gift, I didn't have to purchase beverage products again for three months!

Coin in the fishes mouth:

On a separate occasion, I performed my weekly rounds and picked up our restaurant's products. I had just enough gas to do the job, but I had no idea how I would make it home that night after closing. I had no money. I contemplated asking my in-laws, who lived in the same town where our restaurant was located if I could spend the night so I could open the restaurant the following day.

As these thoughts ran through my head, I remembered the message from church the previous Sunday. The text was Matthew 17:27, where Jesus tells His disciple Peter to go catch a fish, and in its mouth, there would be enough money to pay for their temple tax. I prayed, "Lord, I need a 'coin in the fish's mouth' moment right now." I opened the freight elevator to load our product.

A $10 bill was lying there, and it was enough to buy gas to make it home and back the next day. [6]

No more hose:

When my mom passed away, we had no idea her boss had organized a fundraiser in her honor to raise money for breast cancer research. After they hit their goal, they distributed leftover finances to our family. The amount was just enough to replace our grinder pump so we could use the water in our home again!

Time and time again, when we had no other options, the miraculous happened, and all our needs were met. There were definitely moments when we were beaten down and felt like giving up, but we never lost hope and trusted that God would come through. Miracles still happen, and we're living proof.

Perhaps you want to believe that miracles can still happen too, but you're afraid or uncertain. In Mark 9, Jesus tells a man with a sick child that anything is possible for the person who believes. Here's what happens next: *"Immediately the father of the child cried out and said with tears, 'Lord I believe; help my unbelief!'"* (Mark 9:24, NKJV)

Maybe we choose not to believe in miracles because we don't want to be disappointed. We have believed (or attempted to believe) for so long, and nothing seems to change or improve. We may even sense that the opposite of what we hope for is happening, which

---

[6] This was before you had to mortgage your house to pay for a full gas tank!

makes it easy to feel like our prayers are falling on deaf ears.

Looking back on my life, I remember many times when I believed, and nothing happened. I believed my mom would be healed physically, but this never happened. My situation was similar to that of this man in Mark 9. He had tried many times to find help for his son but was unsuccessful. Something, though, was different this time. Jesus told him to believe, and even though it was a struggle, the man chose to trust in Jesus by asking for His help.

I don't pretend to understand why things don't always happen like we expect. What I do know is that when you don't see God's hand, you can still trust His heart. He has a plan for everything, even if it doesn't seem good at the moment.

If you're going through something, God will use it for good when you keep your faith and hope in Him. No trial is ever wasted. Remember the passage from James I shared before on wisdom? James talks about wisdom in the same breath that he mentions the value of trials. In the verses immediately before, James writes, *"My brethren, count it all joy when you fall into various trials, knowing that the testing of your faith produces patience. But let patience have its perfect work, that you may be perfect and complete, lacking nothing."* (James 1:2-4, NKJV)

Even in the face of struggles, count it all joy because purpose will be birthed out of the struggle. Keep believing.

Chapter Ten: Chick-fil-A

In those days, I began to carve out one day every week to step away from the business. I was still volunteering at the church and serving in pastoral ministry. I knew God wasn't done with me there yet. Little did I know how quickly my time in that role was winding down, and there was no way I could have expected what would happen next.

Being at the church weekly was my place of solitude and restoration throughout all our trials in this season. I could be still in my office without distractions and pray. All that had transpired was preparing my heart to be ready, and I had this sense that something more was on the horizon. I grew restless with the daily turmoil and knew what we were experiencing couldn't possibly be the end.

The incredible generosity of Todd, the Chick-fil-A owner who donated 500 sandwiches for our event, left an indelible impression on me. Whenever my wife and I took our children to his restaurant, we would have this same feeling. In fact, any Chick-fil-A we traveled to with our family left us feeling this way. When the Monroeville Mall Chick-fil-A was still in the food court, I watched every team member serve each guest with hospitality, hustle, and a smile. The desire to own a Chick-fil-A restaurant was a fervent flame in my heart and mind. It was one I simply couldn't extinguish.

After coming home from our restaurant late one night, I shared this desire with my wife. She wanted nothing to do with owning a Chick-fil-A. In all fairness, she thought, "If it's this hard running an operation like ours, how in the world could we possibly run a Chick-fil-A?" She believed that pursuing this path meant amplifying our challenges by a hundredfold. However, this was not an accurate assessment. Kelly's feelings were primarily driven by the fact that we shouldered everything independently without external support. Under the constant weight of our daily struggles, it was easy to see why she held this perspective.

The following week, I was sitting in my office, still dreaming about the possibility of Chick-fil-A. I couldn't shake it. I was so conflicted. On the one hand, my wife was dead set against the idea. On the other hand, it was burning in my heart to apply. In my church office, I prayed and asked the Lord, "What should I do?"

What I heard next was just as clear as the day in my early 20s when God spoke the word "pastor" to me as I drove. The Holy Spirit spoke to me once again. He said, "If you don't apply right now, you'll be making the biggest mistake of your life."

I was utterly flabbergasted! I couldn't stop thinking of Chick-fil-A, but part of me had always wondered if I was being selfish and unreasonable. After God's leading, I did exactly what I heard to do. In that office, I got on my computer and submitted the initial application of intent to own a Chick-fil-A franchise.

I told my pastor what I had done. He was all for it! I went home and timidly confessed my actions to my wife and mother-in-law (who was helping us watch our children one day a week). To my shock, Kelly accepted the news. She stated, "If this is God, we won't have to move." I agreed. God would open a door for us in Pennsylvania, just as He miraculously did so many times before. Two weeks later, I received the official Operator application.

It was January 2013. I sat and stared for what felt like hours at the essay questions that lay before me. I gave much thought and prayer to what I would share with the Chick-fil-A franchisee selection team. It took me almost a month as I labored over the right words to convey what was in my heart. I clicked submit. My Chick-fil-A journey had just begun.

The reply went something like this. "Thank you for your submission. Because of the many applicants, you may not hear from us for three or more months." They were not lying. The opportunity of a lifetime was no joke. I discovered some applicants who had spent five years in this interview process! FIVE! I don't know if you've ever had to interview for that long, but if you desire something badly enough, you'll do what it takes to get there. Anything worth doing in life is on the other side of "hard."

The Process

The Chick-fil-A candidate evaluation is one of the most grueling processes known to man. I once came across a statistic that stated, in terms of probability, gaining entry into the CIA, the FBI, or Harvard might be more achievable than owning your very own Chick-fil-A franchise. I did my utmost to steer clear of reading such content whenever possible. I knew what I was supposed to do and wouldn't let the facts deter me.

In the summer of 2013, I received my first web interview. Things must have gone well because I passed on to the next round. Roughly three months later, I received the invite to Peachtree City in Georgia for my first in-person interview called a "Top Grade." I had dedicated months to preparing for this crucial moment. I meticulously crafted responses for every conceivable question I could think of or unearth through research regarding this process. However, I was entirely unprepared for the first question that escaped my interviewer's lips.

I had arrived the night before at the beautiful resort where all the potential candidates were staying. The following morning, my time had come. I waited anxiously, portfolio in hand, praying silently as my leg furiously bounced. Other candidates sat with me in the waiting area, all with the same look of trying to keep it cool, but in reality, sweating under our suit jackets.

"David?" My interviewer called. As I followed her up the winding stairs to the interview room, I tried to begin with small talk. She wasn't rude or dismissive of my attempt but quickly cut right to the chase.

"What is the biggest regret you have in life?" This was the first question she asked me.

A million thoughts went through my head. "What kind of question is this?! Are you kidding me?! I'm done. It's all over. Chick-fil-A will want to have nothing to do with me." All this flashed through my mind in an instant. I knew I couldn't lie.

"The biggest regret I have is when I was doing drugs, and my dad turned me in to the police," I confessed. I took a deep breath and awaited her response.

"So, were you arrested? Did you receive any charges?"

"No," I explained how God used this moment to shape my life and put me on a path to make a difference for His kingdom. I shared how God brought me into youth ministry, where I could help kids like me growing up. I shared my belief that no moment was wasted because He turns broken things into something extraordinary.

Difficult question after difficult question ensued. Each query was one I wasn't fully prepared to answer. Before I knew it, the hour was up. She said, "I'm not supposed to tell you this, but you are moving on to the next round."

After eight months and this initial in-person interview, I made the "Top Grade!" This meant I was officially an Operator Candidate in the pool of qualified candidates. However, this hardly meant the journey was over. I didn't recognize this then, but I was just entering the gauntlet.

Being Told "No."

"David, would you like to interview for Greensburg, Pennsylvania?"

I couldn't believe it. Six months had passed since my in-person interview with Chick-fil-A in Georgia. It was now January 2014, and I had just received a call from my selector.

"Are you kidding me?!" I thought. The store she was referring to was only 10 minutes from my house. "Yes, I'd be interested!"

I couldn't believe it. I was elated and shared what had transpired with my wife, family, and closest friends. I couldn't contain it. "See, God knew we needed to be here," I declared.

The second in-person interview was scheduled, but the day before I was to fly back to the corporate office, one of the worst winter ice storms ever to hit Atlanta happened. I hoped fervently that my interview and flight would not be canceled. I should've known better and asked them to reschedule. Instead, I kept my plans and made the trip.

After I arrived, I caught the shuttle from the hotel. I was scheduled to have lunch at the Chick-fil-A Support Center (dubbed the "Home Office" or "B52" by insiders) and meet my next round of interviewers. That day, I had the pleasure of meeting some exceptional fellow candidates. We bonded over lunch, exchanged stories, and offered each other encouragement. Remarkably, even nine years later, I still maintain a friendship with one of the other candidates.

We waited outside the offices of the franchisee selection department. I caught a glimpse of that brochure (appropriately placed) warning us of our slim chances of making it through this process on the coffee table. "There it is again," I thought to myself. While some candidates flipped through it, I deliberately avoided reading to shield myself from potential discouragement.

"David Grimm." This time, my name sounded almost sinister when called. I should've expected this after reading the email inviting me to the conversation. It began with, "This interview will be unlike the interviews you've had thus far," and proceeded to subtly forewarn what this encounter would be like.

I was completely unprepared. The interview felt intense, with no room to breathe between questions. It wasn't the typical conversational exchange—I felt the pressure mount with each question as if I were being tested beyond my qualifications. The rapid-fire questions left me scrambling for answers, making the entire experience feel more like an intense examination than a traditional interview. It was overwhelming, and I knew this wasn't going the way I had hoped.

At one point during the interview, I felt my back stiffen. I had barely finished answering the last question, and they were already posing a new, equally challenging question for me to ponder. I interrupted them. "Stop," I said. "If you want me to answer these questions, let me answer." Something had come over me in that moment. I had traveled too far to be treated this way. I would not let these guys rattle me and cause me to forget what I knew was true. I belonged in this room. I had my business plan in hand, and I was unfazed. They weren't inclined to see my plan, but I was determined I would only leave this room with them knowing me and my desire to be in business with this company. I was resolved, although the pressure kept coming.

Soon, the hour was up. They stood up to shake my hand. We exchanged pleasantries, and their demeanor completely changed from the hardened "interrogators" present only seconds before.

"What was going on here?" The question lingered in my head for the rest of that day.

I met with my original selector from since the beginning of this journey afterward to debrief. I was soaked through, and the mental battle caught up with me. I began to question everything that had just transpired.

As I waited for my flight at the airport, I filled my wife and other confidants in on what had happened. "That didn't go well," I told them.

The next day, I was back at Madres Mexican. This decision was now in God's hands. I did everything I knew to do.

It felt like an eternity two weeks later, but the call finally came. "David, we're not giving you the opportunity."

It felt as though time had frozen. I thought this was the right location. If we were to get a Chick-fil-A franchise, surely it was supposed to be near our home! We said this time and again since I had applied. I was finished. I was told, "No," or so I thought. The selector on the other end of the phone continued. "However, you'll remain on the candidacy list. You will be receiving an email soon with the next steps."

I was confused, but I was still in! Internally, the dialogue began, "What now? How did this even happen? This was the worst interview of my life!"

I would learn later that this was a test. What would come out of my character when the pressure was on? Humorously, this situation paled in comparison to the real-life trials we endured to this point. My character had already been tested 100 fold more than this.

I became acutely aware that maybe Pennsylvania wouldn't be in our future. How could I leave my dad after all he had been through? How could I leave my church, where we had invested so much of our lives into the community and where we grew spiritually? How could we leave friends and family and take our children away from their grandparents?

My pastor had challenged me to be open to wherever God would lead. He said, "David, throughout the Scriptures, God called many to leave their homelands for unknown places. He called Abram to leave his home in Ur. He called the Israelites out of Egypt. He may be calling you somewhere else, too. If you want to be where you're supposed to be, you must be willing to go where He leads."

My pastor was right.

Chick-fil-A Experience

Not long after this onerous event, my liaison with the selection department called. She said, "David, I know you've expressed interest in the East Coast. Would you ever consider the Midwest?"

I was finally ready to consider the possibility. I said, "Yes, I will go wherever." I wouldn't let fear of the unknown rob me and my family of this opportunity. When my wife heard the news, she wasn't as receptive. To be fair, our whole support system was still in PA. Our lives were insane, but we had a routine. Our schedule was fine-tuned. How could we interrupt such a good thing?

Everything changed one night after we made another pilgrimage to the front of the church. We needed God's help, wisdom, and direction. After that night, Kelly's heart was ready. I can't say she was happy about the possibilities but was now willing to consider them.

Months later, I received a call from one of the lead selectors in the Midwest. "David, I'm going to be in your neck of the woods, and I would love it if we could connect in person. I hear you're interested in the Midwest."

I emphatically said, "Yes!"

At the interview, I was challenged to get hired at a local Chick-fil-A to learn the ropes and to see what I was getting myself into. I thought, "Sure, why not?" I mean, I had all the time in the world. I was running my restaurant, helping to oversee two other Madres Mexican restaurants a few days a week for our friends who started the concept, serving at the church, preaching weekly, and taking online classes late into the night trying to finish my business degree (as I thought this could only help my chances with Chick-fil-A, especially if it was something they may require). My wife worked another full-time job while also doing our accounting, payroll, and scheduling and working weekly at the restaurant. Oh, and did I mention we had four kids under four years, three of whom were still in diapers?

This could possibly explain why I was having all those shooting pains in my chest, but I said, "Let's go!" I've learned you can do anything for a little while. It may not have been sustainable, but there was an end goal. This wouldn't be permanent.

After an initial meeting to pitch the idea to Todd, the local Chick-fil-A owner, he generously said, "Let's do it. This will be mutually beneficial. You can help me, and I can help you."

We rearranged our routine to accommodate the new plan. I would work for Todd during the week, learning as much as possible about Chick-fil-A. I would be part-time at our restaurant and give our manager more hours and responsibility (which happened to be my wife's late Aunt Linda - the most incredible manager we ever had). I would cut out overseeing all the other Madres and stopped preaching weekly at the church. I would only fill in occasionally. I was all in! So much so that after a couple of months of working with Todd, I was asked to manage his Chick-fil-A location at Westmoreland Mall in Greensburg. I had already had the experience of running my own mall restaurant, which gave me a solid foundation to build upon.

New Chapter

Throughout 2014 and into 2015, I got a crash course in this franchise. I thank Todd for having the vision to allow me to develop with his store and team! I learned a lot thanks to his generosity, patience, and willingness.

This was the right decision for all parties. It allowed the Chick-fil-A franchise team to see I had the capacity, character, competency, and chemistry to be a part of this prestigious business. I was dually able to fill a need for Todd. I treated his restaurant like my own. Despite my experience, learning all the Chick-fil-A systems and standards was quite the learning curve. Running two different restaurant concepts was challenging yet well worth it.

Later that year, the two lead Midwest selectors visited our Mexican restaurant, perused our recipes, evaluated our systems, watched the "Burrito Builders" in action, and tasted all our food. They treated my store like a Chick-fil-A visit. I was glad they were there.

All the hard lessons up to this point and the "MBA of life experience" running our own business made all that we sacrificed worthwhile. After they finished looking everything over, they asked me, "David, where would you like to go?" I thought about it for a moment.

"Are you asking me anywhere?"

"Anywhere," they replied. "I know it's a little bit of a 'bird in hand,' but anywhere."

I visualized all the warm beaches and climates across the US. I thought about Hilton Head Island, our favorite place on the planet. Ultimately, I would defer to their expertise.

I said in all seriousness, "I trust you know where I would best fit. I'm willing to go anywhere." Kelly and I were ready for a new chapter. This season of testing and trials became a preparation ground to be willing. We learned to trust God in all circumstances. This would be no different.

During the next six months, thirteen locations throughout the Midwestern states were presented to me. None were a good fit; ultimately, someone else was chosen for each franchise location.

I was getting discouraged, thinking this might never happen. Then, one day, after months of waiting, I got a call. My selector asked, "What do you think of West Des Moines, Iowa?"

"I have no idea what I think of West Des Moines, Iowa. I don't even know where that is on the map, and I've never heard of it." I replied.

She said, "I want you and Kelly to take a trip there next week and tell us what you think. See if this is a place where you and your wife could raise your family."

Wow, this was all of a sudden getting real! That night, we booked our flights for the following week and arranged for Kelly's mom to stay with the kids. We Googled things to do in West Des Moines.

We arrived at our layover in Chicago. We headed to the terminal for our connecting flight. "Canceled." The airline could only get us a connecting flight the following day. We didn't have time to waste as we only had three days to learn about this town. After much negotiating, the airline finally agreed to pay for a rental car so we could get to our destination.

It was March of 2015. We drove six hours west to our end city but were questioning our decision after only a few minutes. For the entire trip, we drove through what felt like a barren wasteland of nothingness. It was cold, and everything was dead. We saw nothing except for the occasional farmhouse and silo.

After a few hours, my wife started feeling a panic attack as visions of having to drive hours to get to civilization for a Starbucks coffee were playing through her mind. I didn't say it out loud, but I also felt unnerved. "What are we doing?" I thought.

"If this is where they want us to go, I don't think I can do this," Kelly said. I didn't disagree, but I held on to hope until we arrived at our destination.

Finally, we made it to West Des Moines. Signs of life began to emerge on the highway landscape. There was an oasis in the middle of this proverbial desert! We could survive! We could get a good cup of coffee! You may think we are dramatic, but at least we had our priorities straight.

We pulled off Jordan Creek Parkway and loaded our luggage into the hotel. We were greeted with genuine hospitality. We were directed to the hospitality room where, if we wanted anything, we only had to place our room number into the box to be charged. Kelly and I asked each other, "What kind of place is this?"

Where we were from, this stuff would be behind bars under lock and key. Otherwise, it would all be gone! I felt like I was in the movie "Stepford Wives." This kind of Midwest hospitality couldn't be real. It felt unnerving, but in a good way. We received the same experience all over town for the next two days. By the time we left to return to Pennsylvania, our minds were made up. If this is what God had planned for us, West Des Moines is where we wanted to be.

Final Countdown

After two and a half years and at over thirteen interviews (I eventually lost count), plus years of real-life preparation, persevering through trials, and quite literally blood, sweat, and tears, we got the call for the final interview. They even interviewed eight of my personal and professional references to ensure they knew who we were before deciding if they wanted to be in business with us. Every one of our references I talked to afterwards said they were sweating and felt as if they were the candidate in the process when they were finished. It was funny to hear, but this was no joke. This process was intense.

Chick-fil-A would fly Kelly and me to the Atlanta, "Support Center" one last time. It was one week before this critical moment. The only caveat was that we would have to be free of our Mexican restaurant for me to become a Chick-fil-A Operator. We could not own competing franchises and couldn't run another business from another state halfway across the country.

Six months before this, I had been in talks with a businessman interested in purchasing our business. I knew that if we were to be taken seriously by Chick-fil-A, we would have to sell. Three times during negotiations, we were scheduled to be at the lawyer's office to sign the papers for transfer of ownership. He backed out of the deal all three times, leaving Kelly and me distraught and angry for the emotional stringing along. I told him, "Don't ever come see me again." I meant it. I would not be played for a fool any longer.

Kelly and I had no idea what we would do. We both felt like this was the right move, but we had no idea how to sell this place in time.

We had one week before we were supposed to fly to Atlanta. I was working alongside one of the managers at Todd's Chick-fil-A. She had heard our story and was intrigued by the sale of Madres Mexican. By this point, we had lowered the sale price to a "deal of a lifetime."

You couldn't even buy a decent walk-in fridge for the price we reduced it to. She was interested, and Todd was on board.

The day before our flight to our final interview, we received a check and signed the papers for the transfer of ownership. I don't always understand why, but we always seemed to be put in these moments where our faith was tested, and our resolve to trust God for an answer was proved. The last hurdle was crossed, and we ran toward the finish line.

Pre-screening

We touched down in Atlanta, GA. Kelly got to witness what I had experienced many times before. The waiting, anticipation, preparation, fervent prayer, reviewing notes, and the shuttle ride from the hotel to the Chick-fil-A Support Center didn't become easier, even with repetition.

We had a great conversation with our driver and learned all about his life and friendship with Truett Cathy, thanks to my wife. If anyone knows her, they know she can become best friends with anyone she meets for the first time. She IS the life of the party, and you WILL like her immediately. She has a gift.

After we arrived, we were escorted to meet with a few individuals throughout the day for preliminary questions before our final interview. Some of these questions were very intense and personal. Lastly, we were asked if we had sold our business and for how much. We could boldly answer, "Yes! We sold it for the exact amount equivalent to the Chick-fil-A franchise fee."

At the desk of this selector, whom I had sat across many times before, I remembered the words she had spoken to me a year earlier. "David, you look terrible on paper, but when we meet you in person, we see another Truett Cathy. That's who we're trying to replicate in our candidates." This is one of the biggest compliments I could ever receive. He was an incredible man, and I wish we could all live to his standard.

We were finally cleared to proceed to the final interview on the floor above.

Final Interview

All our life experiences and everything we had endured and learned culminated in this final conversation. Here we were, sharing everything with this man. He asked my wife just as many questions as he asked me for half of the interview, and she handled them like a champ. Her answers proved she was ready for this. After all, we were in this together. He had to know my wife wasn't "crazy" and wanted to be a part of this dream. He had to be sure that she was in agreement.

As we were seated across from one another at that little round table in his office, and after he wanted to know the story of my life from birth up until this moment, and of all the stories that we recounted, he asked me one follow-up question. I had heard it through this process before, and he asked again now.

"What is your biggest regret?"

I knew I couldn't answer the way I did years prior when I was asked that question at my first in-person interview. That wasn't a regret any longer. It was a defining moment of change for the good in my life. It was a pivotal moment.

I answered, "I regret not finishing my degree." I had always felt inferior because I didn't finish my college education. God knows it wasn't for a lack of trying. I worked hard to complete it online at night but never quite got there.

He looked at me and completely disarmed me with his answer. "So what?"

"Excuse me? Um, I don't know," I answered in hesitation.

"So, what? I don't believe Truett Cathy ever finished elementary school. Mark Zuckerberg never finished. Bill Gates never finished college. Those guys were all billionaires!"

Suddenly, I felt elevated and confident that I was in good company. Don't get me wrong, my interviewer, Chick-fil-A, and the Cathy family all value education. Truett dedicated many resources to equipping young people with the opportunity to further their education. He shared with me at that moment that I did receive an education. It may not be 100% the same as the previous candidates in my seat, but I had a real-life education. He didn't discount my life because it didn't come with a degree.

With an outstretched arm, he shook mine and Kelly's hands. "Welcome to the Chick-fil-A family. The opportunity is yours if you want it. Congratulations!"

"Yes!" We didn't hesitate at all. Of course, the answer was yes!

The celebration festivities quickly commenced. We got to ring the famed "cowbell," and as it rang out, all that heard came from their offices to congratulate us, take pictures, and enact many more traditions. To ensure I remained humble, my wife will still tell you to this day that she sealed the deal for us in the interview. Thanks again, Kelly!

Chapter Eleven:
Just the Beginning

We made it! In April 2015, I was selected as franchise Owner and Operator of Chick-fil-A University Ave in West Des Moines, IA. We could finally breathe a sigh of relief. One hard-fought battle was finally over, but that moment of comfort would only be celebrated for a short time. Thankfully, it was just long enough to prepare for the next fight that lay ahead.

We tend to forget that life is a journey, not just the pursuit of a destination. We often just want to rush through experiences when they are unpleasant or uncomfortable. I've said it before: anything worth having is never easy. Don't run away from difficulty if you're meant to go through it. Our character is strengthened here, and resolve, perseverance, and discipline are forged. They are used to help us reach new heights of influence, opportunity, and faith if we approach them with care and learning. The journey and all that is gained in the process is the greatest reward!

We are all here in this present life for a purpose. I thought I knew what mine was. Then I moved to Iowa. A quote from my book, *The Never Ending Pursuit*, states, "You and I will never finish the journey to become our best selves. While this may sound discouraging, it's actually a good thing. The goal isn't to arrive at one place. Instead, our objective should be continued growth and transformation each day." I had been so focused on the goal and pursuing this dream that I missed what God was trying to teach and instill in me along the way.

In May 2015, my friend Dan and I packed up a tiny U-Haul and hitched the wagon to the Midwest. I moved to a two-bedroom apartment to get boots on the ground and survey the landscape. We were slated to open our restaurant in August. After weeks of preparation and training in Atlanta, it was finally my turn. I was riding so high on the feeling of excitement that I didn't look back to reflect on where I had just come from. I had learned so much, but I had just written it off as a means to an end. This was mistake number one.

I was never meant to forget all the hardships, trials, and sacrifices that had transpired in the previous years. They were what got us to this moment. I was quickly reminded not to forget the lessons and truths inscribed in my heart and mind.

I was alone. I had no idea how to be alone anymore. Kelly and I needed more money to move the entire family to Iowa. This plan would only happen once I started earning an income when the new restaurant was open. I was living like a bachelor again. Some might think this sounds like freedom, but it felt like a personal prison to me. I was a dad and a husband, and being unable to fulfill these roles was killing me inside. It would've been fine for a while, but the opening got delayed twice due to higher-than-average rainfall that summer, which delayed construction deadlines.

Finally, it was October 7, 2015. Our Grand Opening Day was finally here! It was also my parents' wedding anniversary, which I interpreted as a sign. It was almost as if my mom was there celebrating with us. I believed that even though we were postponed longer than we wanted, God's timing was perfect.

We had been surviving on my wife's income for months, but financial relief was on the horizon. Our friends from Pennsylvania, my family, and the community all came to support us. We celebrated and had a blast, but the festivities were interrupted when we got a call in the middle of the merriment that my son had broken his arm at the playground and was now at the emergency room with grandma.

Honestly, we were unfazed. This was simply par for the course at this point in our lives. We were used to crazy circumstances, and we actually laughed because these were the kinds of life interruptions we were accustomed to. It wouldn't be our grand opening if something like this didn't happen.

After the week-long whirlwind, my family traveled east, and I was alone again. It was ok. I would only be at the apartment each day for a little while because I was spending most of my time at the restaurant while we were building our team and systems. There would be little time to spend with family. Perhaps it would be better this way.

One month down, no paycheck. Two months down, no pay. Three months down, no pay. I know what you might think - new businesses tend to be this way. There are a lot of up-front investments to get things off the ground. Trust me, after three-and-a-half years of running an obscure restaurant and going through many periods of being unable to pay ourselves due to crazy circumstances, I knew this all too well.

Nevertheless, I was starting to sweat this one. I was embarking on the dream of a lifetime and felt like I was back at square one. Since the previous May, I had yet to collect a paycheck. It was now December. I was about to move my wife and kids across the country on January 1, 2016. Kelly's pay was our only income, and we were about to give that up.

You would think after all the other financial crises God brought us through, we would say, "God has this! He'll come through." I could say it in October and November, but when December rolled around, I began to panic. Getting to the destination of the grand opening was not the end-all-be-all I thought it might be. "Do I leave my family behind longer?" I wondered. That was out of the question since we had already rented a house big enough for the six of us in preparation for the move in January. "God, what do I do?"

I sought wisdom and counsel, and I prayed and prayed some more. We hadn't sold our home in Pennsylvania, as my family still needed somewhere to live. It was the fourth quarter, and the installment of the property taxes came due just like always, except we didn't have the money to pay for them. We were late.

I thank God I found the right church when I arrived in town that May. We had been so rooted in Harvest Church, working next to Pastor Shawn and serving with my church friends and family, that I couldn't imagine starting over. Kelly and I prayed we wouldn't waste time church-hopping and that God would lead us to the right place. He answered by leading us to New Hope Assembly of God in Urbandale. The pastors and church members welcomed me with open arms. I felt like I was home.

Thankfully, Chick-fil-A is closed on Sundays, which allowed me to keep attending church amid this quasi-bachelor life. I found it refreshing and renewing. One Sunday, I went forward for prayer because I knew if something didn't happen soon, my family and I would be in trouble. We needed answers.

I didn't tell anyone, but my new senior Pastor, James Weaver, knew something was up. I believe God led him to seek me out. He came to the restaurant one day and asked to meet as long as I agreed to feed him some Chick-fil-A Chicken Strips. Of course, I obliged!

We sat down, and he wasted no time. "Is everything OK? Are you making money?"

My head hung low. No matter how hard I tried, I couldn't make enough money to support my family at my current business. I was working my butt off, but it was happening all over again. I was awarded the number-one franchise brand but couldn't make it work. Self-doubt and deprecation filled my thoughts. "I have no right to be a businessman. I'm a failure." These thoughts replayed over and over.

Pastor Weaver stepped in at the right time. He prayed with me, encouraged me, and told me that he believed God brought me here for a reason and a purpose. This move was no mistake. He encouraged me to hold on and not give up. I knew he was right. I needed to hear it. I wasn't listening through the noise of fear. I was reminded through this godly man to trust God when you can't see His hand.

I finally made my first tiny profit. It was enough to pay for our taxes due in Pennsylvania. However, it wasn't going to be that simple. As soon as I cut that check for myself, I clearly heard God speak to my heart, "Give the whole check."

"What?! But God, I need this check! How am I supposed to do that?!"

I was angry. I had always freely given my tithe and offerings to God's work. I was obedient to the Scriptures in my financial giving. This was the first time in my life that I was angry with God about what He asked me to give. There had been times before when my finances were meager, and I was challenged to give more and reluctantly did so. Never had I been angry about it. I thought, "How could God ask something like this?!"

After my pity party and internal sparring match, I calmed down. I told my wife what God had spoken to me. She said, "Well, you better do it." If I had learned anything in life up until this moment, God would provide. I gave it, albeit reluctantly. And still, I was a little miffed.

Later that week, Pastor Weaver and our co-senior pastor, Jeff Hill, walked into my restaurant. They came to have lunch but then pulled me aside. They handed me a check and said God spoke to their hearts to give this to me. It was the exact amount I had just given from my first profit check! I laughed and said to myself, "God, why do I ever doubt You?!"

Reminders

God was solidifying a few eternal truths deep into my soul. I had reached this perceived pinnacle in my life. It was a goal I had been so intensely focused on for so long, and I had finally made it. When this happened, I let my guard down. I thought that I had arrived and all my problems were now being left behind. Moving to a new area, far away, where no one knows you, has a way of creating this perception.

First, I learned humility. I have not arrived, and I know that I never will. God had allowed me this opportunity, and it wasn't something I could take credit for. If we're not careful, we can think our accomplishments are by our mental prowess and sheer force of will. We aren't as great as we think we are. Remembering where these blessings come from would be in our best interest.

We often read about humility in the Bible. Proverbs 3:34 (NLT) reads, "The Lord mocks the mockers but is gracious to the humble." In the New Testament book 1 Peter, the apostle Peter writes, "So humble yourselves under the mighty power of God, and at the right time he will lift you up in honor." (1 Peter 5:6, NLT) These passages remind me of the importance of crediting and praising God for all the good things in my life.

The second lesson I learned was that this business is not my source of provision. God alone is my Provider. He has given me this opportunity and the ability to run this business for the well-being of my family. He's providing for me as Paul promised in Philippians 4:19 (NLT) when he wrote, "And this same God who takes care of me will supply all your needs from his glorious riches, which have been given to us in Christ Jesus."

This brings me to the last discovery of truth, which is that it's not all about me. It's not about any one of us. We are blessed so that we also can be a blessing to those around us. God gives us the ability to give. We are not meant to hoard all that's been entrusted to us. I've quoted James 1 many times already, and I'll return there for this critical reminder: "And those who are rich should boast that God has humbled them. They will fade away like a little flower in the field." (James 1:10, NLT)

Another passage that comes to mind is from Jesus' Sermon on the Mount. During this speech, Jesus says, "'Don't store up treasures here on earth, where moths eat them and rust destroys them, and where thieves break in and steal. Store your treasures in heaven, where moths and rust cannot destroy, and thieves do not break in and steal. Wherever your treasure is, there the desires of your heart will also be.'" (Matthew 6:19-21, NLT)

For a moment, I had a memory loss and a heart lapse. I forgot who I was and why I was here. Things turned around for us very quickly, though. We became the top-grossing Chick-fil-A across the entire state of Iowa. I was reminded of where my provision came from, and it reinforced the idea that I hadn't accomplished this alone.

We were growing our business, building a trusted team, and learning how to improve daily, but something was still off. I couldn't quite put my finger on it. It was as if I had abandoned my purpose. I knew God called me to pursue this dream, but an empty feeling still lingered. I was pouring my heart into this new venture and felt something holding me back. Like many times before, I prayed and asked God for His guidance to understand what I was feeling.

As it always seems to happen, the answer came from an unexpected source.

Ohmein

One of the benefits of being in business with the Chick-fil-A family is that we are continually given tools, resources, and growth opportunities. We are constantly challenged to be pioneers and never stop dreaming about what's next. It's like living in an alternate reality with no hindrances. The mentality tends to be, "If you can dream it, you can achieve it." Sometimes, it stretches and hurts you, but the growth benefits are exponential. As an example, we are challenged to have personal development plans. Mine includes reading books to continually develop wisdom and insight.

One of the books I added to my library was written by Rabbi Daniel Lapin. I read about him in the book "EntreLeadership" and discovered he wrote "Thou Shalt Prosper." Numerous valuable insights emerged regarding the symbiotic relationship between faith and business.

As I was reading, I read something that stopped me in my tracks.

Lapin writes that the word for "businessman" in Hebrew is "Ohmein." In English, it translates literally as "man of faith."

That was it! That's what I was missing! I felt as though I had forsaken my calling to be a pastor. Lapin's words have messed me up (in a good way) ever since. At that moment, I realized I never stopped being a pastor. My "church" and "congregation" just look different. I'm doing the same things I did at Harvest Church in Pennsylvania, but instead of being inside the traditional four walls, I am now in the marketplace.

We get to run this business and love the people! As a businessman, I am called to be a man of faith daily. I haven't left ministry - just traditional vocational ministry. All that the Lord brought us through and taught us all these years was for this purpose. We're supposed to sell great chicken and minister to people in the process.

As of this writing, we have seen miracles in the lives of our team members, such as the physical healing of an aneurysm, joint pain, cysts, cancer, and many more. We've witnessed many supernatural provisions that were financial and material. Best of all, over 130 of our team members have put their trust in Jesus as Lord and Savior over the last few years. It's called fried chicken evangelism!

God's purpose for my life is to love and care for people the way He does, no matter where I am. Our purpose aligns with the very meaning of the word restaurant. Dan Cathy (the former CEO of Chick-fil-A and son of founder Truett Cathy) shares this teaching with many of us everywhere he goes. The word restaurant is derived from the French word *restaurer*. It means to restore.

Many come into our doors for the physical satisfaction of their hunger, but what they find is so much more. This is a place of spiritual restoration.

I can't get too high and mighty. I sell chicken for a living. I go home smelling like grease and dirty dishes most days, but I wouldn't have it any other way. God is doing big things and will continue to use people like us (yes, even restaurant owners) when our hearts are surrendered.

I'm so thankful I GET to do this because I almost didn't have the chance.

Chapter Twelve:
Pivotal Moments

In John 10, Jesus shares an important truth: "The thief does not come except to steal, and to kill, and to destroy. I have come that they may have life, and that they may have it more abundantly." (John 10:10, NKJV) We need this reminder regularly.

I forgot this promise when I was a young man, and the plan for my life was almost derailed. In Chapter Three, we learned about the ancient war being waged by the enemy of our souls. I nearly allowed this enemy to mar my future. I could've missed my moment. I had a choice in which way I would go, and I selfishly chose the path of destruction. God has much more destined for each of us if we decide to walk in those plans.

Because God loves us so much, He steps in and intervenes despite our foolish choices. As the author of Hebrews tells us, "And have you forgotten the encouraging words God spoke to you as his children? He said, 'My child, don't make light of the Lord's discipline, and don't give up when he corrects you. For the Lord disciplines those he loves, and he punishes each one he accepts as his child.'" (Hebrews 12:5-6, NLT)

Like a good father, God does whatever is necessary to keep us from destroying our lives. If that means using hardship to get us back where we need to be, He will allow it. To be clear, we still have a choice, and sadly, if we ignore God's loving course correction and discipline, we can reap the fruit of our calamitous choices and ultimately lose out on an incredible future.

If we're still here on this planet, that means we still have time to get this right and adjust our path. Cemeteries are full of unrealized dreams and lost potential. So many miss the moments in this life that open up the possibilities to something far more significant. We often choose short-term satisfaction, selfish ambition, and something of lesser quality over an abundant life. We all come across pivotal moments in our lives where we are at a crossroads and can choose which path we will take:

1. We have the option to pursue a path leading to something greater, even though it may be unfamiliar.
2. We can choose our way because we think we know what's best.

Foolishly, I thought I knew what was best and chose the wrong direction repeatedly. Jeremiah 17:9 (NKJV) says, "'The heart is deceitful above all things, And desperately wicked; Who can know it?'"

I have learned how true this is in my own life. I stopped trusting my heart a long time ago, and I've learned to trust the heart of God.

There were weightier moments that could have taken me in the wrong direction. The following are a few of these fork-in-the-road moments throughout my life.

Pivotal Moment #1

I was raised by Barbara and Dennis Grimm, two incredible, godly parents. They loved the Lord, and they loved my sister and me. I came from a good home. Despite not having an abundance, we had everything we needed. You read that when I was a junior in high school at 17, I chose to walk away from my faith. I don't blame my circumstances or the experiences that impacted me. I still had a choice. I allowed myself to be enticed by the things of this world. I wanted to pursue them.

I thank God for all those praying people and my parents who didn't let me off the hook so easily. I thank God for a dad who had tough love and interrupted my path. Being turned into the police caused a dramatic pivot for my future. I thought my life was over, but it was just beginning!

Pivotal Moment #2

You also read about this critical juncture. It was shortly after Kelly and I married in 2002. I was at the facility in the Appalachians working with troubled teens. After three-and-a-half years, I was restless. I knew God had something more in store for my life in that season. I never thought I would return to my childhood church, but there I was, walking in the doors on a Sunday morning. Little did I know that God spoke to the pastor's heart that I was to be his next youth pastor.

What Pastor Shawn heard was unbeknownst to me. Not too long after, I was driving down the road, and out of frustration and feeling stuck, I called out loud, "What am I supposed to do with my life?!" I heard the audible word "pastor" spoken out loud, and I nearly wrecked my car.

After the circumstantial movement of the chess pieces, I became the new youth pastor at the church. I grew in wisdom and knowledge and matured in my faith and character here. I became a family man and learned to care for people from all walks of life. I learned to believe in God for big things and to never stop dreaming! It laid a strong foundation for God to begin building upon.

Pivotal Moment #3

After nine years of vocational ministry, the growing restlessness was back. I recognized God was preparing me for something more again.

I latched on to the vision when my senior pastor prayed for the congregation to have dreams and ideas for starting businesses that could help fuel kingdom work and simultaneously bless our own families. My opportunity came six months later in the form of "Madres Mexican."

The experience was not what I expected, but after three and a half years of operating that restaurant, I was reminded that God is my Provider. I learned how to run a business even in the tough seasons. I learned not to give up and not walk away when everything around me was falling apart.

The Lord used these crucial weighty periods to set us on a course for an incredible future. I learned that not all moments in time are created equal. We learned to recognize when a door of opportunity lay before us and to walk through the door.

Not knowing what lies on the other side can be scary and unnerving. It might be the most demanding terrain you've ever traversed, but who promised that the journey to an abundant life would be a cakewalk?

As we learn in the Proverbs, "We can make our plans, but the Lord determines our steps." (Proverbs 16:9, NLT) Will you walk the steps God has set before you?

Chronos v. Kairos

Do you believe there are moments in time, like the ones I described above, that are more critical than others? That's what these pivotal moments were for me, and these three are just a few examples. I share them so you can learn to take advantage of the life waiting for you.

We use only one word ("time") to mark the passing of the clock, but the Greeks used different words to describe different types of time. The two we'll discuss are chronos and kairos. Chronos refers to seconds, minutes, and hours, but kairos describes important moments in time that rise above the others in importance.

All of us have to pass through chronos. We don't have a choice. We are all bound to the same 24 hours each day. Chronos is best described as the passing of time. We can't ever get this time back, we can't stop it, and we can't avoid going through it.

Whatever we feel about it, we must use it wisely because it will soon be gone. This time is used for preparation. For example, marathon runners train through periods of chronos time to get to race day. Race day would be considered kairos time. Without carefully preparing and using the passing time of chronos, the runner would never be ready for the marked moment of kairos, which is the race itself.

Kairos is defined as the "right time, opportune time, proper time, appointed time." Kairos is a key moment that, if missed or unprepared for, might send your chronological time after this point in a trajectory you don't want. If the runner doesn't prepare, they will not get the opportunity back to run the race in such a way as to win or beat their personal record. Both forms of time are important. You need one type of time to be ready for the other. Chronos prepares you to capitalize on the occasion of kairos.

Will you be ready for that juncture when it comes?

Author Dutch Sheets explains these two types of time in the following excerpt from his blog, "Give Him 15" [7]:

> "Chronos, typically much longer, is planting and tending to the seed; kairos is harvest season. Chronos is mundane, kairos is exciting. Chronos is the investment, kairos is the reward.
>
> As we persevere through difficult times (chronos), if we aren't careful, a mindset can evolve that says life will always be this way. We might begin to believe that the kairos time is never coming. If we're not careful, we lose our expectations, and our faith begins to waver.

We've prayed so long, plowed so long, believed so long, and held on for so long that we begin to live with a 'so long' mentality. Disillusionment then sets in, and our faith is gone.

God wants to shift our mentality from becoming discouraged during these times to realizing the necessity of chronos seasons. We're not losing or wasting time, we're investing it. And if we do so faithfully, the shift will come. Knowing that we are cooperating with God and giving Him what He needs in order to bring the new, we can rejoice over, rather than despise, small beginnings. We won't despair about praying for years with little apparent fruit. Our faith will be based only on the truth of God's Word, unmoved by adversity or delays.

When we are properly prepared and the time is right, God can shift seasons very quickly. Overnight, it seems, He transforms dry places into rivers, barrenness into fruitfulness, and makes a way where there was no way. At the right time, God causes the shift, and change occurs - chronos into kairos. Allow this truth to bring faith and encouragement into your situation.

If we recognize this truth, no circumstance or action will be wasted.

Sometimes, we feel lost, but if we trust God with all the moments of each day that make up the story of our lives, He can create a remarkable story. He is in the business of taking the ordinary, boring, and mundane and turning them into something extraordinary! Maybe you feel that restlessness, like you were created for something more. I want to challenge you to ask Him to get involved. Remember, "'My thoughts are nothing like your thoughts,' says the Lord. 'And my ways are far beyond anything you could imagine.'"(Isaiah 55:8, NLT)"

Had I faced criminal charges at 17, I might've ended up in jail, and my path could have turned out very differently. Chick-fil-A might not have been possible. Had I not heeded God's call to become a youth pastor, I might have never taken the challenge to pursue something greater through business. I never would've learned to care for people like I do now, in addition to so many other important lessons learned. Without "Madres," there would be no Chick-fil-A. My selector said I looked horrible on paper. Taking a leap of faith to open and run our business proved we were entrepreneurs. We didn't just say it – we lived it.

Don't miss out on your kairos moment because you wasted the chronos. Every moment counts. We can't allow ourselves to settle. There's so much more waiting!

Conclusion:
Unlikely Candidate

"Stupid." That's what my first-grade teacher called me. It stung in the moment, but little did she know, God would use that word and experience to ignite a fire within me, a fire of determination and resilience.

I was too "stupid" to back down, too "stupid" to believe I couldn't do it, too "stupid" to accept the odds, too "stupid" to think I would never make it and end up in jail.

My mom always told me I was thick-headed when I was being stubborn. It turns out that this trait can be used for good, not because of me but despite me. As we learn in Ephesians 3:20 (NLT), "Now all glory to God, who is able, through his mighty power at work within us, to accomplish infinitely more than we might ask or think."

I have a knack for dreaming big dreams and thinking to myself, "I can do that." Partially because I don't think of all the hard things that it's going to take to accomplish those big dreams. I just believe it can happen. I equate this to faith like a child. A child doesn't see all the reasons why something CAN'T happen. They just simply believe it can. God has given me faith like a child. Some have called it "stupidity" or "stubbornness," but God has used it in my life to believe Him for the impossible. Luke sums it up this way in his book in chapter 18 verse 17 in the Amplified Version. "I assure you and most solemnly say to you, whoever does not receive the kingdom of God [with faith and humility] like a child will not enter it at all.'"

I want to inspire you to believe in the magnitude of God's plan, a plan that surpasses your wildest imagination. He can accomplish even more than you could ever expect or wish for. No dream is too big for your life if it's God's dream! Step out in faith, and let it be your shield against fear. Don't let fear or the words someone spoke hold you back. Allow them to fuel you for the purpose that you only can fulfill. You can only do so much on your own, but nothing is outside of the realm of possibility for God. Like Jesus says in Mark 10:27 (NLT), "'Humanly speaking, it is impossible. But not with God. Everything is possible with God.'"

God can do anything and will do anything when you place your trust in Him. Hear these words from God spoken to the prophet Isaiah: "For I am about to do something new. See, I have already begun! Do you not see it? I will make a pathway through the wilderness. I will create rivers in the dry wasteland." (Isaiah 43:19, NLT)

You may be stuck. You may have no way out. God can and WILL make a way.

You may have asked but haven't received any answers. Rest assured, God hears you. Your answers are coming at the right time. Persevere. Don't lose heart. Jesus says in Matthew 7:7-8 (NLT),"'Keep on asking, and you will receive what you ask for. Keep on seeking, and you will find. Keep on knocking, and the door will be opened to you. For everyone who asks, receives. Everyone who seeks, finds. And to everyone who knocks, the door will be opened.'"

Keep asking. Keep seeking. Keep knocking.

I'll leave you with the life verse I share at every employee "Vision and Values" training. I've learned in my life that we win every time whenever we don't give up. This verse from Galatians reflects this principle: "So let's not get tired of doing what is good. At just the right time we will reap a harvest of blessing if we don't give up." (Galatians 6:9, NLT)

Never give up. I'm so grateful I didn't.

I was the unlikely candidate, which made me the right candidate for what God did and for what He will continue to do! If you, too, feel unlikely, my story is your story.

Get ready. Your adventure is just beginning…

For more books and weekly inspiration written by David Grimm, visit authordavidgrimm.com.

References

Introduction: Discovering More

Jeremiah 29:11, NLT
1 Corinthians 1:26-27, NLT
Luke 18:27, NKJV
John 10:10, NKJV

Chapter One: Home

Ecclesiastes 3:11, NLT
John 3:16-17, NKJV
John 10:10, NKJV
Jeremiah 29:11, NKJV
Romans 8:28, NIV

Chapter Two: Authoritarian Abuse

https://www.academia.edu/41551933/ST_VINCENT_
S_Saint_Vincent_s_Shaft_Mine_St_Vincent_Shaft_Mi
ne_Village_of_St_Vincent_Shaft_Unity_Township_We
stmoreland_Co_Pennsylvania_U_S_A
Proverbs 4:23, NLT
Romans 7:21, 23-25, NLT

Romans 6:6-14, NLT

Colossians 3:13, NLT

1 John 4:19, NLT

https://www.givehim15.com/post/july-19-2023#:~:text=Father%2C%20when%20Adam%20and%20Eve,human%20race%20and%20the%20earth.

1 Corinthians 15:57, NLT

Philippians 2:5-11

Chapter Three: Paradise Lost

Ezekiel 28:12-15, NKJV

Proverbs 16:18, NLT

Isaiah 14:12, NLT

Isaiah 14:13-15, NKJV

Revelation 12:7-10, NKJV

Luke 10:18, NKJV

John 10:10a, NKJV

Revelation 12:12, NKJV

Chapter Four: The Road Back

Matthew 7:7-8, NLT

"Darth Vader Imperial March," *Star Wars*; John Williams, The Empire Strikes Back: Symphonic Suite, 1980

"Scared Straight!" Golden West Television, 1978

Romans 5:6, NLT

Romans 6:23, NLT

James 5:20, NLT

Chapter Five: Runaway Purpose

Ecclesiastes 3:11, NLT
2 Corinthians 3:18, NLT
2 Corinthians 5:17, NLT
Mark 4:30-32, NLT
Proverbs 15:22, NLT

Chapter Six: Keep Going

"Acquire the Fire," Teen Mania Ministries, Honor Academy
I Corinthians 9:27, NKJV
Galatians 6:2, NKJV
Luke 6:31, NKJV
Jeremiah 18:2, NIV

Chapter Seven: The Call

Galatians 6:9, NKJV
Matthew 19:26, NKJV
I Kings 17:10-14, NKJV
I Kings 17:15-16, NKJV
James 5:17, NLT
Hebrews 11:6, NKJV
Revelation 3:20, NKJV
James 2:17-22, NKJV
Hebrews 11:1-12, NKJV
Hebrews 11:17-32, 34-40, NKJV

Chapter Eight: Big God, Big Dreams

Ephesians 3:20, NKJV
Hebrews 10:24-25, NKJV
Mark 16:18, NKJV
James 5:14-15, NKJV
Proverbs 3:6, NKJV
Proverbs 3:5, NKJV
Psalms 139:1-16, NKJV
James 1:5, NKJV
Hebrews 4:14-16, NKJV
James 1:5, NIV
Exodus 36:1-2, NIV
Matthew 24:35, NKJV
https://www.barna.com/research/what-is-a-tithe/
Philippians 4:19, NLT

Chapter Nine: Season of Testing

Philippians 4:19, NKJV
Psalm 86:17, NKJV
https://www.wtae.com/article/monroeville-mall-suspect-has-juvenile-past/7470040
I Peter 5:7, NKJV
Ecclesiastes 3:1-2, NKJV
Christmas Carol by Charles Dickens
Matthew 17:27, NKJV
Mark 9:24, NKJV
James 1:2-4, NKJV

Chapter Ten: Chick-fil-A

Stepford Wives 2004 Paramount Pictures

Chapter Eleven: Just the Beginning

The Never Ending Pursuit by David Grimm
Proverbs 3:34, NLT
1 Peter 5:6, NLT
Philippians 4:19, NLT
James 1:10, NLT
Matthew 6:19-21, NLT
"EntreLeadership" by Dave Ramsey
"Thou Shalt Prosper" by Rabbi Daniel Lapin

Chapter Twelve: Pivotal Moments

John 10:10, NKJV
Hebrews 12:5-6, NLT
Jeremiah 17:9, NKJV
Proverbs 16:9, NLT
https://www.givehim15.com/post/september-29-2021
Isaiah 55:8, NLT

Conclusion: Unlikely Candidate

Ephesians 3:20, NLT
Luke 18:17, AMP
Mark 10:27, NLT
Isaiah 43:19, NLT
Matthew 7:7-8, NLT
Galatians 6:9, NLT